The Godzone Dictionary

Also by Max Cryer:

Hear Our Voices, We Entreat: The extraordinary story of New Zealand's national anthems

The Godzone Dictionary

of favourite New Zealand words and phrases

Max Cryer

First published 2006; reprinted 2006

Exisle Publishing Limited,
P.O. Box 60-490, Titirangi, Auckland 1230.
www.exislepublishing.com

Copyright © Max Cryer 2006
Max Cryer asserts the moral right to be identified as the author of this work.

All rights reserved. Except for short extracts for the purpose of review, no part of this book may be reproduced, stored in a retrieval system or transmitted in any form or by any means, whether electronic, mechanical, photocopying, recording or otherwise, without prior written permission from the publisher.

National Library of New Zealand Cataloguing-in-Publication data
Cryer, Max.
The Godzone dictionary of favourite New Zealand words and phrases / by Max Cryer.
ISBN 0-908988-74-5
1. English language-New Zealand-Dictionaries. 2. English language-Dictionaries. 3. English language-Dialects-New Zealand-Dictionaries. I. Title.
427.99303-dc 22

Text design and production by BookNZ
Cover design by Christabella Designs
Printed by Brebner Print, Auckland

Max Cryer is a popular public speaker on aspects of language and New Zealand English, through: jhainey@speakers.co.nz.

GODZONE

The term 'God's own country' first appeared in New Zealand literature as the result of an anecdote reported by poet Thomas Bracken after he had visited Melbourne in 1890:

> A recent arrival from New Zealand, walking along Collins Street, Melbourne, a short time since, encountered another Maorilander who holds a good position in the Victorian capital.
> 'Well, how do you like Australia?' enquired the recent arrival.
> 'Oh! It's a wonderful place,' replied the other, 'and I am doing very well here, but I would much sooner live on a far smaller salary in God's own country.'

Bracken used the phrase in an 1893 poem:

> Give me, give me God's own country! there to live and there to die,
> God's own country! fairest region resting 'neath the southern sky.

Subsequently, the Premier, Richard Seddon, used the term publicly, and it quickly went into New Zealand folk history. Although there is evidence that the term had been, and still is, used by other nations, it is nevertheless regarded by New Zealanders as an instant identification of their own country. By 1964 'God's own country' had occasionally been contracted to 'Godzone', the respelling attributed to poet Allen Curnow, and popularised by Bruce Mason and Curnow himself, and it has remained in use, somehow combining irony with a reluctant affection.

Acknowledgements

The author thanks Henare te Ua, Richard Wolfe, Robbie Ancell and Graeme Fisher for their assistance in the preparation of this book.

Introduction

For several hundred years, only the Maori language was spoken in New Zealand. During the 19th century, a strong link with Britain was forged, which remains to this day, influencing many organisations, administrative systems, social structures – and language. Various languages, in fact, since Britain engendered many versions of English, and all of them found their way here. Later came interchange with Australia, and then powerful influences from the United States, by way of television and movies.

But by a process of selection – capricious rather than Darwinian – New Zealand retains those words it regards as fitting, and rejects those it does not, so that a distinctive national language style has emerged.

The selection process does not involve only words and expressions from the English language. When contact between New Zealand and the rest of the world began in the late 1700s, it was clear from the start that some aspects of life in this country could be expressed only in Maori words. And the number of these in general use continues to grow. Since the publication of my 2002 collection, *Curious Kiwi Words,* the number of Maori words now considered an everyday part of New Zealand's vocabulary has doubled: many are included here.

Strong local speech idiosyncrasies have also developed. One is the interrogative rise in pitch at the end of any narrative statement, be it only a single word. Strangely prevalent also is the New Zealand liking for hypocorism – retaining baby-talk into adulthood. When an adult television weather reporter tells his viewers that the day has seen fine beach weather 'and we have pickies to show you', nobody even blinks. It is the same with drinkies, ta-ta, barbie, rellies, Chrissy, drinkies and a dozen others.

In New Zealand, too, metathesis means many words

have their component elements reversed – so etc. becomes *eck-setera*, a dais becomes a *dias*, anemones are reborn as *anenomes*, vulnerable is *vunlerable*, and so on. One television host had to be told that artists were giving a performance, not a *preformance*.

This collection comprises words and terms whose usage is in general confined within New Zealand. Some were created here; others may have originated, and been forgotten, elsewhere, but they remain in currency here.

A dialect can be defined as 'a form of speech particular to a district, a variety of language with a non-standard vocabulary in relation to the language family to which it belongs'.

The Godzone Dictionary is a study of, and tribute to, the dialect of New Zealand.

Max Cryer
January 2006

A

Adam – since Adam was a cowboy Referring to a time long ago, or covering an extensive period. This version of the expression and another version referring to a well-known former premier, 'Since Dick Seddon died', are variations on a very old British expression: 'When Adam was an oakum boy in Chatham dockyard'. Besides the adaptations indicated above, other variations exist, e.g. 'Since God called the chickens home', and 'Since the Lord had measles'.

ae *Maori* Used in the same way as English 'yes', to indicate agreement.

afghan This crunchy, chocolate biscuit, usually containing cornflakes, and topped with rich chocolate icing and a walnut, has been popular in New Zealand since the 1930s. The name apparently refers to the dark colour.

afternoon tea A mid-afternoon break, either from work duties or as a purely social occasion, usually including snacks of varying levels of elegance, and some kind of non-alcoholic drink.

aggro *abbrev.* A combination of aggravation (made worse, intensified) and aggression (over-readiness to attack), this contracted abbreviation came into use in the 1960s to indicate annoyance and exasperation. The meaning of aggro has both widened and weakened: it can indicate either a potential street fight, or something as minor as a person being a few minutes late, thus causing aggro to the person waiting. *Bernie couldn't play rugby on Saturday – he damaged his hands after some aggro in the street on Friday night.*

agribusiness A term referring to commercial land use as a business, interacting with service and supply organisations. It can also be heard as a recognition that farming of any kind, besides being a vocation, must also generate income and use the same techniques as other businesses.

a into g *abbrev., informal* Arse into gear, either describing one's own burst of activity, or sometimes an instruction to someone else, to get started and become active. *He'll never finish painting the house by Easter unless he gets his a into g very soon.*

ake, ake *Maori* Signifies eternity, for ever. Maori language intensifies or enlarges a description by doubling the word, so ake, ake is forever and ever, as in the 'Maori Battalion Marching Song': Ake, ake, kia kaha e! – Forever and ever, be strong!

All Blacks New Zealand's official representative rugby team. They wore blue at their first outing in 1884, but changed to black in 1893. There has been no clear evidence confirming why they became known as All Blacks, apart from the simple fact that their uniforms were that colour. The first known printing of the name was in the Devon *Express and Echo* in September 1905: 'The "All Blacks" as they are styled, by reason of their sable and unrelieved costume'. A belief that the name came from a British provincial newspaper's typographical error – 'blacks' rather than 'backs' – has never been proven.

all get out To a high degree, achieving total effectiveness. *When Mum got dressed for the wedding, she was as glamorous as all get out.*

All Whites The New Zealand men's international soccer team (Association Football).

amber liquid A popular colloquialism for beer. Whether through some overhang of temperance puritanism or an uncharacteristic desire to make the language more colourful, beer is often referred to by other names. Rather than say the word itself, suds, sauce and turps were used as informal replacements – and often the noun was dropped altogether: to 'have a few' or 'sink a few' are common New Zealand expressions.

Anglican A Christian denomination, sometimes referred to as Church of England or, especially in the United States, Episcopalian.

ankle-biters Small children. The term is believed to be of New Zealand origin, but was made prominent by Australian entertainer Barry Humphries. An equivalent is rug rats.

Antipodes Before the 1860s, British people used Antipodes (from the Greek for 'opposite the feet') to mean the whole of the Southern Hemisphere, but with the growth of colonisation in Australia and New Zealand, the term became confined to those countries. Interestingly, Australasia is opposite Spain, not Britain, on the globe.

Anzac *abbrev*. Australian (and) New Zealand Army Corps. In 1914 Lieutenant-General Sir William Birdwood took command of the part of the British Army, including Australians and New Zealanders, that would land at Gallipoli in Turkey on 25 April 1915. Birdwood is credited with coining the acronym Anzac, having seen the initials stamped on boxes of supplies and documents pertaining to those forces. The infamous Gallipoli campaign, in which the first Anzacs took part, killed 2721 New Zealanders and wounded 4752 others.

Anzac biscuits A recipe for Anzac cakes was published in 1915 and six years later a recipe for Anzac crispies united the ingredients and method which, by 1927, had become known as Anzac biscuits. The key ingredients are golden syrup and rolled oats: coconut and walnuts are optional extras and there have been occasional variations such as the chocolate-coated version created for the millennium in 2000.

Anzac Day This New Zealand public holiday on 25 April commemorates the Gallipoli landing in 1915. Soldiers from both sides of the Tasman marked Anzac Day with memorial services in 1916 and two years later the same idea surfaced in Sydney. In 1919 the Prince of Wales attended an Anzac Day march in London and the day was officially recognised in New Zealand legislation in 1920. The word Anzac cannot be used in any commercial activity without approval and its date must remain 25 April, regardless of which day of the week it falls on. Since the First World War the term Anzac has widened to include all who have given their lives for their country.

Aorangi *Maori* Cloud in the sky, but freely translated as cloud piercer. It was the original name for New Zealand's highest peak, Mount Cook, which is now officially know as Aoraki/Mount Cook. (South Island Maori customarily use the letter *k* where North Island Maori use *ng*.)

Aotearoa *Maori* Although acknowledged as the Maori name for New Zealand, this is not necessarily the country's original name, as it is most unlikely that these islands had any name at all in the early days of their habitation. Abel Tasman called the country Staten Land, but that lasted for only a year. The words Nieuw Zeeland and Zeelandia Nova had crept onto maps by the mid-1600s and have lasted. The usual Maori transliteration, used in the Treaty of Waitangi, was Nu Terani. The spelling Niu Tireni also occurred in the latter half of the 19th century, after which that name vanished completely. Aotearoa first appeared in about 1860 and though the meaning is generally given as 'land of the long white cloud', the exact meaning and origins have never been clear.

A & P show *abbrev*. An Agricultural and Pastoral (Association) regional festival event with a strongly rural and agrarian focus, which includes exhibitions of livestock, produce and machinery, trade displays, educational material and fairground activities. The first A & P Association was formed in 1843, to improve crops and agriculture and show livestock and machinery. By 1908, there were over 100 A & P Associations throughout the country. Actively involved in rural postal, telephone and schooling services, the associations were non-political and paid increasing attention to holding A & P shows, which can be a major event in many communities, often referred to simply as the Show, or, in Canterbury, Show Week.

Arbor Day 5 June, on which date tree planting is encouraged. (*Arbor* is Latin for tree.) The idea of an annual tree-planting day originated in Nebraska in 1872. There were initially plenty of trees in 19th-century New Zealand but those who understood that the vegetation was being destroyed by settlement, instigated an Arbor Day at Greytown in the Wairarapa in July 1890. Pine trees and spruces were planted and Queen Victoria sent her good wishes. Two years later the government established an official annual Arbor Day, in August. Then in 1972, to align New Zealand with World Environment Day, the date was moved to 5 June.

Arikinui *Maori* Great chief, with connotations of spiritual, rather than military, leadership. It is the correct title for the Maori Queen, Dame Te Ata Irangikaahu.
(See **Maori Queen**)

aroha *Maori* Love. The term covers many shades of meaning – affection, sympathetic warmth, romantic love for a person, all-embracing love for a family, love of a wide group of people, of a nation, of a landscape.

arohanui *Maori* Literally, great love, this is often used within a personal greeting or farewell, or to signify warm affection towards a large body of people or land.

artic., articulator *abbrev.* Short for articulated truck, a long vehicle consisting of a driving unit, with one or more hinged sections behind it. Known variously elsewhere as a semi, a semi-trailer, an 18-wheeler and a big-rig.

arvo *abbrev.* Short for afternoon. Sometimes extended to s'arvo for 'this afternoon'. A recognised Australian word by the mid-1920s, it has since become familiar in New Zealand.

asphalt Semi-solid mineral mix of bitumen and inert matter, used as waterproofing and also found in some fungicides and paints. Mixed with gravel, it is commonly used for road surfaces.
(See **metal** and **sealed road**)

aue *Maori* An exclamation in which the vocal colour used, and the context in which it is spoken, can encompass emotions as varied as surprise, affirmation, despair, congratulation, acceptance of inevitability and sometimes satisfaction.

auntie *abbrev., informal* Besides its standard application as an affectionate version of the formal aunt, the term auntie has a more general use within Maori social structure. Any adult female relative, connection, in-law or close family friend can be referred to as an auntie. Within Maori families, auntie carries a certain cachet, denoting someone who is older and wiser than the younger family members. New Zealand's Maori television epitomises their position perfectly – a programme featuring a panel of mature women who give advice in answer to viewers' letters is named *Ask Your Auntie*.
(See **bro, cuzzie, rellies**)

Australasia The combined areas of New Zealand and Australia. The word seems to have arisen from an error. In the late 18th century the French word *Australasie* was sometimes used to refer to Australia and Asia and over time it came to signify Australia and its outlying islands, which included New

Zealand. Once New Zealand had its own separate identity – in the late 1800s – Australasia came to mean the distinct nations of Australia and New Zealand, plus their respective outlying islands (such as the Chathams or the Aucklands). By the end of the 20th century the word was little used in New Zealand and seldom across the Tasman.

Avondale spiders   These large Australian Huntsman spiders were imported accidentally during the 1920s, when butchers in the Auckland district of Avondale took delivery of a new commodity – a gas refrigerator. The spiders arrived in the packaging and were soon keeping themselves warm near the machinery that drove the fridge. Because they ate flies and bugs, the butchers encouraged the spiders by leaving out little bits of mince when their premises were closed. During the 1930s the butchery was pulled down, and the resident spiders had to move on. Avondale spiders, now a local curiosity, are not poisonous, but they make a curious spitting noise when upset.

away with the fairies   A state of living in fantasy and daydreams. Can describe a project which is being earnestly promoted but does not appear to be based on reality. Sometimes, away with the pixies. *Harry is keen on a dodgy investment company offering a 37 per cent profit – either Harry or the company is away with the fairies.*

away laughing   To have a project (or problem) under control, to be on the way to success, and winning. *If we can get the new house roof on before the rains begin, we'll be away laughing.*

B

bach A usually simple, even makeshift and often small, weekend or holiday house, often lacking such amenities as a garage or laundry. The word, which has been used in New Zealand since the early 1900s, probably originates from the verb to bach, meaning to live like a bachelor – cooking and carrying out domestic tasks in a rudimentary way. Once an affordable commodity, coastal baches are becoming increasingly expensive as urban New Zealanders seek a place by the sea. Particularly in the south of the South Island, people call a bach a crib.
(See **crib**)

backblocks Anywhere that is a long way from a city, areas considered distant from mainstream or urban living. The word comes from surveying, which divides a potential housing or farming area into blocks. Since 1852 land far from the coast, a settlement or even a house, was referred to as a back block. Joined together as backblocks, the word was common throughout most of the 20th century and is even used rather derisively of anything clearly non-urban. *Bernie and his wife have left their city apartment and moved out of town. I wonder how they'll like living in the backblocks.*
(See **sticks, the**)

back-hander (1) In sports, a stroke effected from the reverse direction to that considered 'normal'. (2) An illicit financial transaction: either an unofficial and unacknowledged so-called bonus provided for carrying out a project, or slight overcharging, so that a small portion of the profit can be slyly pocketed. *The sale of his company showed only a small profit, but there were several back-handers to sweeten the deal.*

bags that Staking a claim before someone else. Thought to have been used by British poachers, the term arises from the notion of putting something securely in a sack and guarding it as one's own. Although 'I bag that' is grammatically correct, the expression is always 'I bags that'. The term is more widely used in Australia and New Zealand than Britain, especially by children.

bald as a badger Completely bald. There are no badgers in New Zealand and they are not bald. British in origin, the phrase is part of the expression 'bald as a badger's bum', because it was widely thought that bristles for shaving and artists' brushes were plucked from that area of the animal. Also occasionally heard is 'bald as a coot', referring to a bird whose white-fronted head gives an impression of baldness.

bang A brief way of intensifying a statement, e.g. *She put the playpen bang in the middle of the living room floor.*

banger See **sausage**

barbecue Cooking food (especially meat) over direct fire, usually outdoors. The word has been in use with more or less its current meaning since the 18th century and there are two theories about its origin. One says that because an entire animal was often cooked over a fire, barbecue arises from the French phrase *barbe à queue* – from head to tail. Others believe that barbecue derives from the West Indian word *berbekot*, describing the framework of strong green branches on which Haitian natives roasted or smoked meat. Spanish travellers and explorers borrowed this word, pronouncing it as *barbacoa*. Taken to North America, *barbacoa* became the word for the grid on which a whole ox was roasted, and gradually became barbecue. The word now refers not just to the structure on which the meat is cooked but also to the food and the social occasion of gathering to eat outdoors. New Zealanders often talk about a barbie and advertisers often take the abbreviation further, to BBQ.

Barber The bitterly cold wind which sometimes blows around Greymouth on the West Coast of the South Island, and is said to be sharp enough to shave a man.

barney A fight. It is derived from an ancient British and Irish dialect word meaning a lively journey, a lark. During the 19th century, the meaning shifted towards displaying anger and by the 1930s barney in New Zealand meant a fight. (Speculation that barney was Cockney rhyming slang, derived from Barney Rubble – trouble, or Barney Fife – strife, has no validity, since the word existed long before those two television characters appeared in 1960.)
(See **stoush**)

barrack To make noisy and public comment, often concerning the progress of a sports match or meeting. The term works two ways: it can describe either support for the situation, or jeering condemnation, and both can sometimes occur simultaneously. The word has little to do with military quarters – those barracks are derived from a Spanish word meaning tent – but appears to have arisen in Irish dialect, referring to loud boasting and bragging. Both uses – loud approval or loud criticism – have been common in Australasia since 1897.

bash A spree, an active social occasion, often involving liberal use of alcohol and pursuing the pleasures of company and noise. The term is derived from the old Scottish expression 'on the bash', meaning a drinking marathon. *When the neighbours won a bunch of cash in Lotto, you could hear the bash three blocks away.*

bathroom A room with a bath and wash-basin. The word came into use when New Zealand lavatories were outside the main part of the house, and possibly had little or nothing to do with water. When the lavatory became part of the house, it tended to be placed in a little room on its own, separate from the bathroom, and called the toilet, the lavatory or sometimes the loo. Later, the lavatory and the bath were often out in the same room. The American custom of saying bathroom when they mean lavatory or toilet can cause confusion in New Zealand.

beaut, beauty *abbrev.* of beauty or beautiful. Expression of approval, indicating excellence, rather than traditional beauty. It can be used to describe an idea, a person who provides something necessary, or anything else that makes a good impression. Often preceded by 'little' which, in an eccentric contradiction, intensifies the beaut into 'big'.

Because it was there This was the answer Sir Edmund Hillary gave when asked, in 1953, why he had climbed the world's highest peak, Mount Everest. Surrounded by other mountaineers, Hillary knew they would know, as the reporter did not, that this was not an original reply but the words used in 1924 by a famous earlier mountaineer, Sir George Leigh Mallory, when he was asked the same question. Mallory had delivered the phrase with impatience: a silly question deserving a silly answer.

Beehive The now-official name for New Zealand's Government Office Building in Wellington. Sir Basil Spence's original design for the building was somewhat jokingly compared to the shape of a Beehive and the name stuck.

bench The flat working area in a kitchen or DIY area. In other places this is known as a counter, but New Zealanders use that word only for the flat area in a shop where customers are served by staff.

berm The formal and official word (as used by city councils and so on) for the strip of grass between the footpath and the road (or the boundary and the road, if there is no footpath). Berm is related to brim: both words come from an ancient

Scandinavian word meaning edge. Berm, originally used to describe part of a castle, seems to have survived only in New Zealand, although most Kiwis now say grass verge instead.

bickies, bikkies (1) A childish abbreviation for biscuits. (2) An informal term for money, usually large amounts. Sometimes heard in the negative – not having any bickies, i.e. having no money – but more usually as big bickies, of something like a major lottery win. The opposite – small bickies – is also possible, though less common. Variants like stiff bickies and tough bickies, meaning bad luck or tough circumstances, are frequent.

biddy-bid A creeping plant native to New Zealand, with burrs and many-seeded fruits with small hooked spines. The word is a corruption of the Maori name piripiri. Biddy-bids are a serious nuisance to farmers, since prickly burrs caught in sheep's wool reduce the value of a fleece. Biddy-bids are also a nuisance when caught in clothing or the fur of domestic pets.

biff *sometimes* **bish** To hit, or to throw. This is derived from an old English word signifying an interruption or interjection.

big gun A person of notable skill or in a position of importance and authority. The term is often applied to an expert shearer, but also applicable especially to those carrying out activities where physical effort and dexterity are required and visible. It can (rarely) apply to more contemplative skills if the person being described is particularly successful and important.

The expression originated in the 1800s, when an impressive firearm – a great or big gun – was associated with the image of an important person. The related term 'big shot' arose much later, during the 1920s, when the imagery of urban gang warfare became widespread. In some contexts the word big has eroded, and just gun is sufficient, whereas big has been retained in big shot and in associated terms with the same meaning: big wheel, big cheese, big kahuna, big enchilada.

'In the gun' is slightly different. A descendant of the informal British term describing someone drunk, it now means being in trouble of any kind.

big-noter A person who consistently draws attention to their own success, wealth, high-ranking contacts and superior ideas. *Since she got that top job in television, Amy has become a name-dropper and a big-noter.*

biker Devotee of either cycling or motorbiking.

bikie Motorbike devotee who probably belongs to a gang.

bill Document displaying the cost incurred. In a restaurant, the written-down price of a meal. Americans use 'check' in this context, which can cause confusion in New Zealand since it sounds like cheque.
(See **docket**)

bill of lading Document specifically describing goods being transported. The word 'lading' is derived from an ancient German word *hladan*, meaning a load or cargo.

billy A cylindrical metal utensil, usually with a lid, used for carrying food or liquid, and sometimes for outdoor cooking. The billy was sometimes the tin that once held a kind of meat called *bouilli*, which became bully beef. New Zealand households once used billies to collect milk, gather fruit and boil water for making tea outside. As musterers, trampers and hikers know, basic bread, cakes and stew can also be made in a billy. Boiling the billy is an informal way of saying making tea and keeping the billy boiling is a way of saying that you are making sure everything keeps going.

bitser *abbrev.* of bits of this and bits of that. The word is very often used as a jocular description of a dog whose ancestry is unknown but clearly colourful.

bivvy *abbrev.* of bivouac – a (temporary) position in which to settle. The term arose originally from the Swiss word *Biwacht*, meaning extra watch – a citizen patrol in city areas. The term was adopted by the military for an all-night watch and came to mean a night encampment, usually without tents. The shortened version is used by New Zealand bush-walkers, trampers and mountaineers to signify a short-term resting place – either just the position itself, or the tent or hut built there.

Black Caps New Zealand's national representative men's cricket team.

Black Ferns New Zealand's representative team of women rugby union players. Teams of rugby-playing women first came under the jurisdiction of the New Zealand Rugby Union in 1989. The national side was originally known informally as the 'Gal Blacks', until the formal name Black Ferns was acquired from a previous owner who held the copyright, and registered in 2000. The first Women's Rugby World Cup was an unofficial event in 1991, but subsequent events have been organised by the International Rugby Board. New Zealand teams have competed in three World Cups, winning the title in 1998 and 2002.

Black Sox New Zealand's representative men's softball team.

Black Sticks New Zealand's national representative men's and women's hockey teams.

block The head, based on its shape and solidity compared with a similarly sized lump of wood. The image arises from the British use of block, since the 17th century, as informal reference to the head – along with bun, loaf and nut. All of these are understood in Australia and New Zealand, but by the start of the 1900s, block was being preferred.
(See **do your block, knock someone's block off, use your block**)

bloke An ordinary man. The word comes from the Shelta

language, spoken by itinerant tinkers travelling through Britain in the 18th and 19th centuries. Little used in Britain, the word became popular in egalitarian Australia and New Zealand. Its feminine form, blokess, is believed to have been invented by witty New Zealand writer Jim Hopkins and was widely popularised by the late comedian Billy T. James.

blow (1) A stroke of the handpiece into a sheep's wool, when being shorn. (2) *Abbrev.* of fly-blown, indicating that food or a stock animal has suffered significant deposits of blowfly eggs. Other senses retain a connection to the literal meaning of blow – the forceful motion of a fast passage of air, e.g. in such combinations as blow off – to boast and brag; blow up – to show extreme annoyance, anger as destructive as a bursting volcano; blow out – either a burst tyre, or a bout of reckless activity (spending money, for instance, or eating); blow me down – expression of complete surprise, as if the information could push someone to the ground.

blow that *abbrev.* of 'blow that for a joke', indicating vehement disagreement, disgust, exasperation or dismissal. It is sometimes considered a milder substitute for 'damn that', as damn is still considered a curse in some countries and very offensive. *Blow that for a joke – I'm not taking the risk.*

There is also 'blowing up', from military descriptions of bombing, which indicates that whatever is being suggested is being firmly rejected.

bludge Passively managing to benefit from other people's efforts rather than one's own, getting others to do or provide essential things. To bludge means to impose on, to shirk responsibility or hard work, or to borrow excessively, to sponge. The word's ancestor is bludgeon, a heavy stick, wielded by a person called a bludgeoner. The word bludgeon is still occasionally sometimes used as a verb, describing an attack on someone with a blunt object.

Gradually, bludgeoner became shortened to bludger, and the meaning softened. The word has been used on both sides of the Tasman since about 1900. *My brother never pays for a holiday – he contacts relatives in distant places, invites himself and bludges off them for several weeks.*
(See **cadge, dole**)

blue, bluey (1) A mistake, believed to have arisen as an *abbrev.* of bloomer (originally used to describe a mistake which became obvious, easy to see – like a flower in bloom). (2) Disagreement or a fight. Since trouble and argument can lead to fisticuffs and a resulting appearance in court, in Australia such a brawl became referred to by the colour of the court summons, which came on blue paper. The term later transferred to New Zealand.

blue fit An explosion of irritation or anger, often because of an unexpected happening, or unwelcome information. The term may have an unfortunate origin, since it is believed to be derived from an insensitive description of someone suffering an apoplectic seizure.

bluff (1) To pretend, in order to confuse someone. This meaning originates from the Dutch *bluffen* – to boast (especially about one's hand, in a game of poker). (2) To become lost or frustrated, as in the case of sheep musterers who accidentally drive their flock to a steep cliff beyond which they cannot proceed, and must turn back.

bobby calves A calf which is older than four but younger than seven days and has been fed solely on whole milk. Its navel must be dry and it must be able to stand on its own. The term was officially and strictly defined in New Zealand in 1982, and bobby calves can only be sold as such for slaughter (or for rennet, which comes from their stomach) when they meet these criteria. The word calf is generally used of a young cow or bull up to 12 months old. The bobby part comes from a

Cornish dialect word for a very young calf.

bobsy die   A commotion, an upheaval, a confusion. The origin is an ancient English expression Bob's-a-dying. By 1800 the meaning of commotion and grief surrounding death had changed and the term was used by naval men to describe a joyous, often drunken commotion.

The original phrase has had several changes – Bobs-a-dial, Bobs-a-dilo – before emerging as bobsy die (or bobsidie), usually preceded by kicking up. *When Marion heard that Frank was going to arrive an hour late for the wedding, she kicked up bobsy die.*

boil-up   (1) Preparing hot water and making tea. The term usually applies to outdoor preparation, using a billy and a fire. (2) A popular meal among Maori, consisting of meat and vegetables cooked together in stock. The ingredients are basically similar to those of a traditional stew, but often also include green leaf vegetables such as puha, and since the mixture is rarely thickened, the consistency is closer to heavy soup.

Bombay Hills   A range of hills that forms a convenient geographic southern boundary to what is perceived as Greater Auckland. The general area, originally a little settlement 50 kilometres south of Auckland, was named by its founding inhabitants after their immigrant ship, *Bombay*, which brought them to New Zealand in 1865. As Auckland spread, its outer suburbs reached almost as far as the Bombay Hills. Because the landscape south of the hills remained noticeably rural, in contrast to what many other New Zealanders decried as Auckland's glitzy metropolitan lifestyle, early in the 1980s these people began referring to Auckland as north of the Bombay Hills and the rest of New Zealand as south of the Bombay Hills.
(See **JAFA, RONZ**)

bonnet The lift-up cover over the engine of a car. Other countries, especially the United States, call it a hood. New Zealanders lift the bonnet; Americans pop the hood.
(See **boot, bumper, mudguard**)

booai See **up the booai**

bookings To make a future arrangement for the services of a person such as a tradesman, or to ensure a seat in a theatre or plane. Overseas visitors can be confused by the term, thinking it concerns reading, or making bets with a bookmaker. More common for them is the word reservation.

boonger, boonga, boong An offensive term sometimes, but rarely, used to refer to a Pacific Islander. It originated in Australia during the 18th century, derived from a native word there meaning anus, and was used by Europeans referring to Australian Aboriginals.

boot The storage section of a car, usually at the rear, with a separate door. The use of the word in this context is probably connected to footwear, since both uses relate to a protective cover. For Americans, a car boot is a trunk.
(See **bonnet, bumper, mudguard**)

boot sale A gathering of cars parked in an open space (e.g. school grounds) with their boots open to display a selection of small goods, usually of a domestic nature or collectables, which are for sale. Boot sales are often used as a fundraising exercise. The car owners pay a fee to participate.
(See **garage sale**)

boots and all To act with a strong sense of purpose, letting nothing stand in the way. *Bill didn't tackle the garden clearing half-heartedly – he was in, boots and all.*

bot (the) An informal way of describing any infectious illness, most commonly a heavy cold, of the severity usually known as flu. The term comes from rural life, where an unpleasant botfly produces parasitic larvae which develop inside the bodies of horses and sheep. A beast carrying the visible eggs on its hide has the bots and the eggs have to be scoured off. Abbreviated to the bot, the term became applied to human illness.

bottler   A term of great approval and admiration, referring to a person, thing, concept or outcome of a project. The reason for using the word is obscure, but may relate to the British term 'bottle', meaning courage, which itself is derived from rhyming slang: bottle and glass meaning arse, a synonym for bottom which, in turn, has an ancient association with courage. Hence, a bottler – a person of courage – became a figure to admire. As with little beaut, calling someone or something a little bottler intensifies the compliment.

Boule Blacks   Informal name for New Zealand's international representative petanque team.

bowser   A retail dispensing centre for petrol. The name comes from an American petrol pump producer called S.F. Bowser Ltd: many of the Indiana company's products were used in New Zealand after 1919 and bowser came to refer to the pump itself, or the business establishment where bowsers could be found. The word was gradually replaced by petrol pump.

box of birds   Feeling happy, exhilarated, fit and cheerful. First found in print in 1943, this phrase is thought to have originated in the New Zealand military during the Second World War and has remained popular largely because of its pleasing alliteration. After about 1980, the modification box of budgies developed; another variation is box of fluffy ducks (or even box of fluffies). *Martin was laid low with bronchitis, but he's recovered now and he's a box of birds!*

boy racers   Young men who drive their cars on public roads in unnecessary exhibitions of speed with an irresponsible disregard for their own and other drivers' safety or convenience. Another ingredient is often present: extremely loud in-vehicle music.

braces Elasticised strips over the shoulders with grip ends, designed to hold belt-less trousers in place. These are sometimes known elsewhere as suspenders.

brassed off Irritated and cross, having reached the end of patience. The term is believed to have a military origin, when reprimands were issued by senior officers, aka brass hats.

bro *abbrev.* of brother. The use of the abbreviated form originated in Britain during the 17th century and was later borrowed by Black Americans referring to each other as soul bros. During the late 1900s the term became current in New Zealand, particularly among Maori. Besides straightforward filial connection, the term has a wider set of meanings: Maori families often contain a foster child, a stepchild, a half-sibling or even a legal cousin. Calling such a person a bro can show a close link even without an actual blood relationship. The word is also used for members of a group such as a gang and, more widely, to refer ironically or jokingly to all Maori people.
(See **cuzzie, rellies, auntie**)

buck rat An indication of health and energy, usually in fit as a buck rat. The expression is similar to fit as a fiddle or fit as a flea but rather more physical.

buckshee Free of any monetary charge, or gaining an unexpected extra. The word is derived from the Arabic *baksheesh*, meaning a gift, a present. Picked up by New Zealand soldiers in Egypt during the First World War, the word has been spelt in a number of ways. Buckshee was also used in a military context to describe a wound that was not disabling but meant the injured man could be sent home. The first meaning is much more common these days.

buddy A friend, in a more casual way than a person with whom one has a long-lasting association (more likely to be called a mate). The word is derived from a baby-talk version of brother.
(See **mate**)

bugger An exclamation of irritation. Long ago in Europe the word Bulgarian was used to describe a group of mavericks, weirdos or outsiders. It crossed into English as bugger, used to describe male homosexuals. Gradually the word changed its meaning to a more general, though vulgar, exclamation of surprise, shock or vehement irritation. In 1999 the word became comically acceptable in New Zealand thanks to a popular television commercial.

There are several expansions: bugger-lugs – based on an old ancient nautical expression that was not necessarily offensive, related to bugger grips aka sideboards, sideburns or side whiskers; bugger off – go away; bugger up – to confuse or render inoperative; bugger all – a small amount, insufficient; bugger that – I don't like it; bugger me – I'm surprised.

built-up area Urban district consisting mainly of buildings, and not notable for trees, parks or breathing space.

bull *abbrev.* of bullshit, information of low value and credibility, or none. Variations include bull-dust (nonsense), bull-artist (someone who tells unbelievable stories) and bullshit as a descriptive expletive indicating that the matter under discussion is beneath contempt. At least until the 1970s the word bullshit was considered unacceptable when used in public. The title of then social activist Tim Shadbolt's biography *Bullshit and Jellybeans* was received with some disapprobation when published in 1971, and one year later visiting academic Dr Germaine Greer was fined $40 for saying the word at a public meeting.

bumper The horizontal bar at the back and front of a vehicle

which protects against accidental impact damage. It is also known by some as a fender.
(See **mudguard, boot, bonnet**)

bun fight   A jocular description of any social function at which food is available as an adjunct to the function's main purpose. The term is sometimes used as a deliberate put-down in reference to a grand event, such as a parliamentary reception: a bun fight at the Beehive.

bung   Broken, not functioning as desired. Its origin is a Yagara Aboriginal dialect word meaning dead.

bungy (bunjie, bungee)   An adventure activity which became popular c.1980, whereby long rubber straps are attached to the ankles of people who then jump from high places, and bounce back up and down several times. Voluntary high-jumping, with restraining cords preventing impact with the ground, originated as a manhood ritual on Pentecost Island, Vanuatu. The idea was adapted by young entrepreneur A.J. Hackett, who turned it into a New Zealand tourism phenomenon. Modern bungy jumping is a sophisticated money-making enterprise involving complex gear and jumping sites as exotic as the Eiffel Tower.

The word seems to have begun as injie, an informal name for an India rubber pencil eraser. Most of these were short and thick, like a barrel bung, so the word drifted towards bunjie or bungy. A version of the same word also surfaced as Navy slang for a physical training instructor. In the mid-20th century the word was used to describe strong rubbery-elastic cords with a hook at each end, used to secure baggage on a bicycle or car.

bush   The preferred New Zealand word for territory which is heavily treed. Bush is derived from the Dutch word *bosch*, meaning woodland. New Zealanders avoid woods or forest, though the latter is used to describe areas of exotic trees,

especially *Pinus radiata*, which have been deliberately planted. Native forest can describe more substantial areas of indigenous trees but bush is common too.
(See **go bush, forest**)

bush baptist   A person of strong religious belief whose desire to convert others is inclined to oversell the advantages of their particular faith. In some cases that faith can be of an anti-establishment kind, unrelated to any known and recognised forms of worship.

bushed   (1) Tired, worn out. (2) Frustrated. (3) Puzzled. All forms of the idiom relate to being caught or lost in the bush and unable to find a way out before nightfall.

bush lawyer   (1) Informal name for a New Zealand native vine, *Rubus cissoides* (known in Maori as tataramoa), so called because the thorns of the vine are as difficult to escape as the entanglements of the legal system. (2) When referring to a person rather than a plant, the term means (a) a lawyer who involves someone in a legal complexity from which it is difficult to escape, or (b) an unqualified person who, simply by observing the process of law, offers opinions on legal matters. The second meaning is more widely used.

bush nightie   Informal comic name for a bush shirt which, when it was launched, contravened convention by being designed to wear outside the trousers.
(See **Swanndri**)

bushwhacker   In the late 1900s the term referred to a forest worker. Over the ensuing decades it developed to include forms of behaviour and a make-do living style which would be normal in outback conditions but could seem comic in an urban context. *He's hospitable enough, but the house is a real bushwhacker's place.*

busso   The person travelling with a touring sports team who alerts members about bus departures, and rounds them up for travelling on.

Buzzy Bee A fat, surprised-looking wooden bee, with little wheels and a string to drag it along the floor. The wheels make the wooden wings go round, and also activate an internal metal strip that makes a clacking sound. The toy was launched in 1947 by Auckland brothers Hec and John Ramsey, designers and manufacturers of toys including Peter Pup, Richard Rabbit and Playful Puss. The Buzzy Bee enjoyed impressive commercial success and became a standard feature in almost every New Zealand family home. It has since acquired iconic status as an amusing but unique example of New Zealand inventiveness. The Buzzy Bee, its name patented in 1975, achieved international prominence when, on a visit to New Zealand with his parents, the infant Prince William played with one and was recorded by a myriad of television cameras. Although the toy has been made in China since 1985, it remains an essential part of New Zealand folklore.

by hokey Exclamation of surprise or affirmation. The expression comes from the Irish term 'be the hokey', introduced into New Zealand during the 1870s by Irish writer Thomas Bracken, and first seen in his journalistic pieces written under the pseudonym Paddy Murphy. For many decades from 1946 onwards, as by hokey, the expression became the signature of radio and television broadcaster Selwyn Toogood.

BYO Acronym for bring your own, referring to alcohol. Originally, in the 1950s, BYOG – Bring Your Own Grog – the expression was common especially on university party invitations. The G was quickly lost. Restaurants were using the initials by the late 1960s to indicate that they were not licensed to sell liquor, but could serve alcohol brought in by a customer. BYOG is related to a similar overseas acronym, PBAB: please bring a bottle.

C

cabbage tree A medium-height tree, *Cordyline australis*, ti in Maori, with a slim trunk and characteristic crown shape. In pre-European days, Maori steamed the main root of the tree, then baked it. The result is very palatable because a sugary substance in the root structure crystallises during cooking. As European visitors did as early as 1769, 19th-century settlers cooked the soft young leaves from the centre of the tree's head as a substitute for cabbage – hence the tree's popular English name. (In fact sailors in 1773 thought it tasted more like sweet fresh almonds.)

New Zealanders, so used to this familiar part of the Kiwi landscape, can be surprised to see cabbage trees in the centre of the English seaside town of Torquay: in Britain they are imported as Torquay palms, though they actually belong to the agave family.

cab sav *abbrev.* of cabernet sauvignon, a thick-skinned red grape widely used in the Bordeaux region, and elsewhere (including New Zealand), to make a wine of the same name.

cactus, in the In trouble, often financial. To a New Zealander, any landscape naturally containing cactus is alien to their own – and slightly threatening. As a stand-alone, (the) cactus can simply mean a distant and isolated place. Being in the cactus conveys difficulty and the prospect of a possibly painful exercise in order to become free. *Bartlett's farm was quite prosperous until the flood in the middle of the growing season, which has left him in the cactus.*

cadge To borrow, though probably not with a concept of returning. This meaning arose in Britain during the 19th century but survives far more commonly in New Zealand. Often expanded to on the cadge.
(See **bludge**)

califont A domestic water heater. Califont is a trade name, registered at the beginning of the 20th century, for a heater that was originally powered by gas, but later by electricity. The derivation is Latin – *caldus* meaning hot, and *fons* meaning source of water. The 'f' was sometimes changed to 'ph', perhaps because it evoked a more elegant image.

candy floss Tinted sugar, spun in a heated mechanical bowl to enlarge its bulk, producing a cloud-like, usually pink, abundance of sweet and slightly brittle fluff, usually mounted on a stick for convenient eating. Known elsewhere as cotton-candy or fairy-floss.

capping An informal name for the graduation ceremony marking the fact that a person has satisfied all requirements for a university degree and has become a graduand. A dignitary presents the hatless graduand with a certificate of their achievement. At that point the graduand puts on a traditional mortar board hat (sometimes called a trencher) and becomes a graduate. The ceremony is not obligatory – a graduation diploma can simply be sent by mail.

Several festive activities customarily arise during the university's capping week, some informal (often called 'stunts') and some more regulated: a street procession, a special 'capping magazine' and sometimes a comical theatre revue.

Captain Cooker A type of wild pig. Captain James Cook is reputed to have introduced domestic pigs into New Zealand during the late 1700s, and those which escaped and became feral developed into the breed correctly known as Captain Cookers – a short lean razor-back pig with dangerous tusks and an aggressive personality. The term Captain Cooker is also often informally and casually applied to any wild pig.

carbonettes Heavily compressed egg-shaped dry carbon fuel, also sometimes known as brickettes. Although no longer so popular indoors, as fireplaces become less common, they can be used to fuel outdoor braziers and barbecues.

cardy *abbrev.* of cardigan, a knitted coat-like outer garment, usually long-sleeved and either buttoned or zipped up the front. The garment originated with James Thomas Brudenell, the Earl of Cardigan, who, in 1854, developed a buttoned, collarless knitted coat to wear in the Crimean War. The 'Cardigan Bodywarmer' was initially worn only by men. Women did not commonly wear knitted outer garments until the beginning of the 20th century. The abbreviation especially has acquired a pejorative and jocular connotation, a pointer to lack of style.

cark (it) To die. The term arose in Australia, apparently from a combination of sources – the caw sound of a crow (reminiscent of a human death croak), plus the sound of carcase, and both possibly influenced by a British dialect word 'cark', meaning fret and worry, eventually intense enough to be fatal.

cattle stop A small moat across a gateway with spaced narrow horizontal metal rails at ground level, from one side to the other. Animals with hooves cannot walk across because of the gaps between the rails.

caucus The meeting of political representatives in order to co-ordinate policy. Caucus comes from the Native American Indian Algonquin tribe's word *caucauas*, meaning adviser, counsellor. The anglicised version of the word has been used in the United States since the mid-1600s and in New Zealand since 1876.

cervena A trade name for New Zealand deer-meat which has been raised on a farm rather than caught in the wild (that meat is called venison). Invented in 1993, the word combines three elements: 'cer' comes from *cervidae* (Latin for deer), the 'ven' refers to venison, and the final 'a' conveys A grade.

chain See **drag the chain**

Chateau cardboard Bulk wine, without elegant ancestry, sold in cardboard boxes with a plastic lining. The expression was coined in the 1970s, and broadcaster Sharon Crosbie made it famous.

cheeky Impertinent, bold, saucy, impudent. In other places the quality might be described as sassy, showing chutzpah or gall. Cheeky could describe an overtalkative child, a quaint poster, an eye-catching outfit or perhaps an unexpected combination of foods.

cheerio A very small spicy sausage, usually bright red. The name was instigated by Colin Munro, the affable New Zealand manager of Huttons Meat Co., who registered the name in 1933. Often served as a party snack, cheerios are usually cooked and served with toothpicks and a bowl of tomato sauce. In other countries they are called cocktail sausages, maybe wieners or weenies, and Australia calls them little boys.
(See **sausages**)

chemist Retail shop incorporating a dispensary for prescription medicines and medical supplies, which also sells non-prescription health products, cosmetics and bodycare preparations. A New Zealand chemist shop bears little resemblance to its American counterpart, a drugstore.
(See **dairy**)

cher or **cher cher** An expression of approbation widely used among Maori. Its origin is obscure, but it is believed to have arisen from a custom in Australian vernacular of describing many things as champion, which became abbreviated to champ. When the gimmick caught on in New Zealand, champ became abbreviated even further into just ch or cher (with possible echoes of choice and cheers). It is widely used as an affirmative either in addition to, or in place of, hello, thank you, good luck, well done, cheers, bon voyage, I agree, congratulations.

Chesdale cheese A brand name for a processed cheese developed by Butland Industries. It was discovered, in 1968, that the public had a low regard for processed cheese. Chesdale, however, was a good cheddar cheese, especially made for processing and it became the focus of a popular advertising campaign, involving two animated characters called Ches and Dale, created by well-known New Zealand artist Dick Frizzell. Their song was composed by Terry Grey, and sung by Brian Borland and Gordon Hubbard from The Yeomen with Peter Carter on guitar. The jingle became enormously popular – The Yeomen included it in their performances for years – and most New Zealanders of a certain age can sing it without thinking twice.

> We are the boys from down on the farm,
> We really know our cheese
> There's much better value in Chesdale,
> It never fails to please.
> Chesdale slices thinly,
> Never crumbles, there's no waste
> And boy it's got a mighty taste –
> Chesdale cheese:
> It's finest Cheddar, made better.

chicken Originally, the juvenile of a hen, fowl or poultry. American-inspired aggressive marketing, contriving to bestow youth, blurred the line between juvenile and adult, and usage widened so that the word chicken included ever maturing candidates. By the end of the 20th century, a size 16 bird weighing 1.5 kilograms was being classified by its marketers as a chicken, while the words hen, fowl and poultry disappeared altogether from labelling or retail usage.
(See **chook** and **silly as a chook**)

chilly-bin An insulated container in which articles (usually food) can be kept cold. The bin is easily transportable, and for several hours maintains a cool internal temperature without need of electricity or refrigerants. Most usually the chilly-bin is a lightweight oblong chest with generous polystyrene lining, intended for taking food on picnics or to the beach. The name Chilly Bin is a trademark registered by Skellerup Industries in 1974.

chip (1) Pieces of chopped potato which have been deep-boiled in fat and eaten hot. Sometimes erroneously called French fries, though they are neither French nor fried. (2) Very thinly sliced potatoes deep-boiled in fat, sealed in air-tight bags and eaten cold – sometimes also known as crisps. (3) A small and insubstantial container, meant to hold a portion of berry fruits during brief transport.
(See **crisps, punnet, pottle**)

chippie Informal term for a carpenter or builder.

chocolate fish A fish-shaped chocolate-coated marshmallow confection. Popular in New Zealand since 1930, chocolate fish are often used as comic prizes in fun events.

choice If something meets with approbation it can be described as neat, cool or choice. Sometimes the meaning can be deliberately ironic.

chokka *abbrev.* of chock-full, full to capacity. It is derived from the 17th-century term choke-full. During the 20th century military personnel adopted the term chokka to mean disgruntled, often accompanied by a hand gesture to the neck indicating up to here – so still full. Sometimes spelt as chocker, or chockers.

chook Vernacular diminutive for hen. Derived from the British vernacular 'chook' and 'chookie', chook is closely related to the affectionate dialect word 'chuck', all derived originally from chicken, and often heard in regional speech such as that on *Coronation Street*. In New Zealand chook describes any domestic hen, regardless of age, and the cry 'Chook-chook-chook' was a familiar rural or suburban sound when it came feeding time. (In Australia a prominent politician referred to his press conferences as feeding the chooks.) Sometimes the term was extended beyond life and into the oven: roast chook. (See **silly as a chook**)

Chrissy *abbrev*. of Christmas.

chuck To throw. Originally regarded as a slang or childish word, not used by adults or educated people, it has some related variations: chuck off (make fun of); chuck up (to vomit); chuck it in (to relinquish, give up); chuck away, chuck out, give it the chuck (to get rid of, throw somewhere else).

chuddy Chewing gum, considered casual and usually juvenile. Originally chuddygum, it was common in New Zealand throughout the 20th century but has since fallen out of favour and been replaced by the American abbreviation, just gum.

chuffed, chuff (1) To be pleased, filled with joy or pride. There is disagreement over the word's origin but the 16th-century chuff, describing fat cheeks, seems to be fairly likely. Since then chuffed has altered its meaning from pleased to displeased, and then back again. (2) In New Zealand, chuff also means bottom, as in the admonition against laziness, Get off your chuff.

clapped out A general term for anything or anyone who has reached the end of their effectiveness. The origin of the term is probably related to the clap (gonorrhoea): someone so afflicted would be sexually incapacitated. London club cyclists in the 1920s used it to describe their exhausted riders. The Royal Air Force disseminated the term during the Second World War, referring to machines – particularly planes in those years –

that had served their time. The term is more widely used in New Zealand than in Britain.

Claytons An unconvincing substitute, an imitation. In 1980 a television commercial for a non-alcoholic Australian drink called Claytons used the slogan, – 'Claytons – the drink I have when I'm not having a drink'. Claytons quickly caught on to express disillusion with anything that was not what it seemed to be. The drink itself had a very short life, but the word remains in sporadic use.

clobber, clobbering machine To be severely beaten, or destructively criticised. The word, which arises in historic English, is thought to be echoic – it sounds like the action of beating. Both the Royal Air Force and the navy used clobber and clobbering to describe heavy bombing or successful submarine torpedo attacks.

In New Zealand, clobbering came to mean that people are expected or pressured to conform with and submit to accepted standards. British MP and author Austin Mitchell, who lived in New Zealand in the 1970s, wrote of the Great New Zealand Clobbering Machine.

clock In the appropriate context, clock substitutes for odometer on a car, especially in such terms as wind the clock back or turn the clock forward – altering the travelled distance already registered. When considering a second-hand car, the question is often asked: *How many miles has it got on the clock*? (Although New Zealand uses the metric system, the imperial term mileage is still sometimes heard.)

clout, to have Possessing either power or influence, in commerce, sports, government, entertainment or any activity with a hierarchy. Derived from the Dutch *kluit*, a lump, which during the 15th century moved into English as clout. A basic meaning of a blow with the hand or a hard object, a thump, still remains, but this began to take on a figurative connotation in the mid-20th century. Because clout meant that someone was being beaten by another person more physically powerful, it gradually became a synonym for major influence or power.

Coast, the *abbrev*. Of the West Coast. New Zealand has over 15,000 kilometres of coastline and reference to any section of it is usually preceded by some geographic clue. But particularly in the South Island the Coast is regarded as shorthand for the West Coast of that island, between Karamea and Haast. Those who live in the area are called Coasters.

cobber A friend. The original British dialect word cob, meaning to take a liking to someone, travelled to Australia, then expanded to cobber and was in use in New Zealand by the 1890s.

coconuts An informal, usually insulting term referring to people from the Pacific Islands. It can be acceptable when used by Pacific Islanders themselves but otherwise is best avoided. The basic word, coconut, comes from the Portuguese word *coco*, which means grinning face – a version of which can be seen on a fresh coconut. (There is no connection with cocoa, which derives from the South American native word *cacao*, the name of the plant whose seeds are ground into chocolate powder known as cocoa.)

collywobbles General illness, but in particular upset stomach and/or diarrhoea. Derived from the Latin *colon*, the bowel, with wobble added, the word is of British derivation, and widely used in New Zealand.

colonial goose Boned mutton, filled with savoury stuffing, roasted and served with potatoes, usually at Christmas. The practice arose when British pioneer settlers discovered that there were no geese in New Zealand – and Christmas was in summer. Unwilling to abandon old traditions, they evolved a new Antipodean version. Apart from the name, it has nothing to do with geese at all.

come again? Please repeat what you have just said, i.e. explain it more clearly. *She told me how to install the new computer program but I got confused, and said, 'Come again?'*

come at To present a concept or possibility, usually disbelieved. Often preceded by don't. *When Hansen claimed he couldn't pay my bill, I said, 'Don't come at that – I know you've got money in the bank.'*

come away The plants will grow. It is usually said once seeds have been planted, or when larger plants have been pruned and will sprout fresh growth.

compere The person who introduces the various sections of an event, commentates on happenings and announces guest speakers etc. An equivalent to the similar term master of ceremonies or MC.

compo *abbrev.* of compensation. In general this is a payment by an establishment such as the Accident Compensation Corporation (ACC) or employing body to replace or make amends for a loss or injury. *The building accident put Albie off work for six weeks but he got compo from the ACC.*

contractor The person initiating the project and paying those engaged to work on it. On the same basis as employer (the person who organises and pays the workforce) and employee (those working for and being paid by the employer) you might expect contractee, but New Zealand usage avoids this and describes both roles with the word contractor.

convert, conversion In New Zealand law, a euphemism for stolen. The correct legal usage is 'converted to one's own use': being found guilty in court of stealing a car is referred to as a conviction for car conversion.

cootie Adaptation of the Maori word kutu, meaning head-lice.

corker Estimable, outstanding and remarkable. It is a long-used word (it appears in the novels of P.G.Wodehouse) but the origin is unclear; corks are not involved. It first appeared in print in New Zealand in 1862. It is sometimes preceded by beauty – a beauty corker is especially remarkable and worthy of praise.

corrugated iron Zinc-coated iron sheets put through rollers, causing a series of regular ridges and hollows that provide maximum strength. An 1828 British invention, it became particularly useful for roofs, fences, water tanks and a variety of farm buildings. It is highly visible in New Zealand, for whole buildings as well: world-famous scientist Lord Rutherford began studying physics and chemistry in a corrugated-iron lecture hall at Canterbury College in Christchurch. These days it is a popular building material for modern homes and artist Jeff Thomson is famous for his corrugated iron animals.

corry (by, or **pai)** sometimes also **korry, gorry, kolly, korrie** Maori variation on (by) God, often used deliberately as a euphemism in circumstances where saying God would be deemed inappropriate.

cow cocky Dairy farmer. Cocky is short for cockatoo, the Australian bird with a Dutch-Malaysian name. City dwellers regarded the more bleak open spaces of the countryside, preferred by farmers, as fit only for cockatoos. Cocky can be qualified depending on what the farmer deals with – e.g. cow cocky, goat cocky, deer cocky – but in New Zealand a cocky is invariably associated with cows.

cracker (1) Expression of approval applied to a person, thing or situation. The term arose in Britain during the 1400s, originally meaning boastful and loud, but slowly changed to mean, by the 1800s, a fine fellow or an outstanding set of circumstances. In New Zealand the meaning may have been drawn from the sound a skilful whip wielder can achieve when flicking the fine thread at the end of a whip lash, causing an impressive cracking sound. (2) Money or any sort of valuables – usually expressed as a negative. *He was fired from his job and was left without a cracker*. The imagery comes from a thin colourless biscuit of the same name.

crack hardy (hearty) To maintain a show of courage or strength in the face of difficulties, even though the concealed reality may be quite the opposite.

creek A stream or (small) river. Derived from the ancient Dutch word *kreke,* it originally meant an inlet or a bay, which is what Captain Cook may have meant when he wrote of mooring in a creek. In the 1600s British immigrants in America began using creek to describe a running stream or small river. In the 18th century European Australians used the word in the same way and by the early 1800s it had spread to New Zealand for any waterway smaller than a river. Stream is seldom used. Brook, beck and rill are never heard, though burn appears occasionally in the south of the South Island, where a strong Scottish influence survives.

crib A weekend or holiday house of fairly simple proportions and facilities, usually in a rural setting, in Otago and Southland. The word comes originally from a German word *krebe* meaning basket, and crib slowly developed a variety of meanings, including a small cottage. This usage was brought to New Zealand by early European immigrants, and has remained in the southern South Island. It is one of the few examples in New Zealand of a distinct linguistic regional variation: other Kiwis call a crib a bach. Those who own cribs are sometimes known as cribbies.
(See **bach**)

crikey dick An expression of anger, surprise, shock or despair combining twinned substitute euphemisms crikey (for Christ) and dick (for the devil). The expression is an example of the age-old practice of wanting to exclaim the name of a religious figure, while trying to avoid offence by doing so. Accordingly, many similar-sounding words developed, which could be said with impunity: Oh my goodness rather than Oh my God; cripes and crikey rather than Christ; gee and jeepers rather than Jesus; golly and gosh rather than God.

crisps Thin slices of potato, cooked in fat, salted, dried and packaged in foil then eaten cold. Chips are thicker slices of potato served hot, directly from being cooked in boiling fat. (See **chip**)

crispy Fresh, firm and brittle, or orderly and neat, concise and pithy. Usually seen as crisp in English, though crispy was used during the 17th century, the word comes the Latin *crispus* meaning curled. After an American breakfast cereal company reintroduced the earlier spelling for an animal-shaped breakfast cereal called Crispy Critters in the late 1950s, the word was taken up by food writers and television cooks, and from 1960 crispy virtually replaced crisp.

crook Dishonest, financially shady, or unkind fortune (a crook deal); unpleasant (a crook day); being ill (feeling crook); disturbed (a crook night); badly constructed (crook roof); dishonest (a crook partner); inedible (crook food); anger (to go crook); deterioration (going crook); or bad advice (to put someone crook). All the meanings relate to the word's origin, the ancient Norse *krokh* meaning a hook – something bent out of its normal shape. In English it became crook, with various associated developments such as a shepherd's crook and crook-back. Eventually crooked was applied to dishonest people, then shortened to crook.

cross-lease A legal arrangement, whereby the several

occupiers of what in effect is one property, are registered in joint ownership, each leasing their property from the owners of the other portions of the property.

crud Accumulated dirt or the semblance of it, undesirable residue, either actual or metaphorical. The word is a curious example of reversion to an ancient spelling: crud is the original spelling of curd. *Their flat was untidy and always looked really cruddy.*

crutching Removal of wool, which often holds accumulated deposits of dried faeces, from between a sheep's back legs. (See **dag**)

cuppa *informal, abbrev.* A cup of tea. The phrase can also indicate a work break, socialising, a rest – often with something to eat as well. If you are asked to a cuppa after a formal Maori ceremony, generous amounts of food may be involved.

curly (1) A term of approbation indicating high approval. *They put us in front row seats— extra curly!* (2) Identifying a problem, especially a question which is difficult to answer. *I had trouble at the job interview – some of the questions were really curly.*

custard square A popular square slice consisting of soft sweet custard sandwiched between baked pastry and topped with icing. Also sometimes known as a vanilla slice.

custard, turn to A metaphor indicating that a project has fallen apart and degenerated into a mess. Custard is formless, shapeless and difficult to control.

cut (1) Finished. (2) Drunk, tipsy. These two meanings carry the same connotation as when a slaughtered animal is useless once its throat has been cut. In a mild paradox, (2) is usually heard as half cut – indicating that a person is only halfway to complete drunkenness. (3) A share – providing portions as from cutting into pieces.

cut lunch A light midday meal provided from home, often sandwiches accompanied by a piece of cake or something sweet, and fruit. A cut lunch is often carried by farmers, schoolchildren and workers who either prefer home-made food or may be some distance from any commercial food supply.

cutty grass *informal, abbrev.* (often among children) of cutting grass, especially toetoe and sedges with a sharp leaf edge.

cuzzie A cousin. An expansion derived from the old English informal term coz, meaning cousin, as used by Shakespeare. Nineteenth-century Maori were largely unfamiliar with European familial structures. They adhered strongly to a knowledge of aristocratic succession and lineage, and in closer domestic situations were accustomed to a complex system including adoptions, half-siblings and children being raised by grandparents. Maori therefore often used the English word cousin to describe all types of relatives because it satisfied European expectations and prevented embarrassment and further questioning. The word became widespread. Young Maori quickly turned the tables by deliberately using the word in wildly improbable and eventually comic contexts. Cousin developed into cuzzie, and its use was popularised by famous comedian the late Billy T. James.

Cuzzie is often shortened to cuz and there is also an expanded version – cuzzie bro – by which Maori jocularly refer to almost anyone else Maori, related or not.

(See **bro, rellies, auntie**)

D

dag (1) Dry dung hanging from the rear area of a sheep. It is believed to derive from an old British word similar to tag – a hanging piece, as in price tag. (2) A lively person. This dag is differently derived, from *degen*, a kind of sword, which after the 17th century was occasionally used to describe an artful fellow, a knowing blade, someone daring. The meaning has not changed much in modern New Zealand: a bit of a dag is someone slightly bold and probably amusing as well.
(See **rattle your dags**, **crutching**)

dairy A small shop, licensed to sell mixed groceries, milk, eggs, dairy products and perishables during and after normal trading hours. The name originates in the days when perishables such as milk and eggs were delivered to city households from a dairy. By the late 1930s the name shifted over to describe the small shops stocking such produce, even though they also sold other items. In the United States, a similar shop is sometimes called a convenience store, or a drugstore, which means it sells drugs and liquor, two commodities which very few New Zealand dairies are licensed to stock.

The word dairy also retains its normal meaning in New Zealand – that is concerning milk and products derived from milk and the industries associated with them.
(See **chemist**)

daks Men's underpants. The name originated from Simeon Simpson's tailoring firm, established in 1894 in London. In 1934 his son devised the self-supporting beltless trouser, and contrived the name daks from dad plus slacks. In some places the word daks has become a shorthand for trousers of any kind (in Australia, for examples, trackpants are trackie daks) but in New Zealand the word has definitely moved under cover.

dally *abbrev.* of Dalmatian, loosely applied to any peoples of Slavic descent. People from Dalmatia (which became part of Yugoslavia) began arriving in New Zealand in the late 1800s, many to dig for kauri tree gum, which was used for a variety of purposes. Initially dally was mildly pejorative, mainly because of suspicion about anyone non-British, and the dally interest in, and skill at, making wine later created the expression dally plonk (see **plonk**). Recognition of their work ethic and citizenship qualities gradually increased respect for immigrants from the various states of Yugoslavia, and dally became a term of affectionate regard. Slavic families often cheerfully said it about themselves.

dawn raid In 1974 government officers, attempting to monitor and prosecute those people breaking the immigration laws, began to make unexpected and very early visits to households in which overstayers – those who had exceeded the time period stated on their temporary visas – were thought to be living. (See **overstayer**)

dead loss A project, idea or job, in which the amount of effort expected is in no way compensated for by an equivalent reward. The term can also be applied to a person whose aptitude is in the negative range. The prefix dead functions as an intensifier: the loss is finite, absolute and definite.

dear Expensive. Besides its usual meanings of beloved, precious, appealing or surprising, New Zealand has retained one of the less common meanings of dear, namely expensive or costly. When an object, a shop or a service is described as 'very dear' it is not being mentioned with affectionate regard, but rather that its prices are high. *I buy vegetables at the quick turnover Chinese shops. The supermarket ones have become too dear.*

deck (1) On deck – being available, awake, contributing work to a project. (2) To deck – physical attack, sufficiently powerful to bring the other person to the ground. *Someone in the team insulted Fred's wife, so he decked him.*

de facto A man and woman living together as if they were husband and wife, but without being legally married. The basis of the term is the legal distinction between *de jure* (in law) and *de facto* (in factual existence). The term began, properly, as an adjective – a de facto relationship – but has become a noun: She was his de facto. It is not a familiar term in many places outside New Zealand, where terms like common law wife might be used. And within New Zealand, de facto is gradually being replaced by the less harsh-sounding partner.

designated driver A person who, by agreement, drinks no alcohol at a social function so he or she can drive the others home. This practice has developed in the face of a rising road toll and the resulting heavier policing of drunken driving.

ding Minor damage to the body of a vehicle. The word is also sometimes used to refer to the accident that caused the damage. Its origin is possibly echoic, reproducing the sound of the original impact on metal, like prang, though ding has long existed in English meaning a blow and including the sound made when a bell is struck.

dingbat A friendly indication that someone is slightly foolish, zany, amusing or crazy in a harmless way. The person being described has the same level of sense as a bell, whose only function is to be struck, and the image is enhanced by the addition of bat, bringing to mind another expression of eccentricity – bats in the belfry.

dinkum Honest, true, fair. From an ancient English dialect word meaning work. In the 19th century the word travelled to Australia where, besides its meaning of work, it gained an extra connotation of suggesting work to full capacity.

Gradually the concept of honesty replaced the image of work, and dinkum came to mean truthfulness and honest dealing.
(See **fair dinkum**)

dip out To fail, to be unsuccessful, to lose, not to make the required grade. Possibly of Australian origin, where it appeared in print in 1965, it is frequently used in New Zealand.

Ditch, the The Tasman Sea, between New Zealand and Australia. Within New Zealand the 2000 kilometres of sea and three and a half hours' flying time between the two countries is seldom referred to it by its formal name, and Australia uses the name even less. Australia has been referred to as 'across the Ditch' since the early 1900s. A former Premier of New Zealand, Richard Seddon, once said that there were over a thousand reasons why New Zealand would not join with Australia – one for every mile between them.

divvy (1) *abbrev.* of dividend. A payout from a bet, or financial speculation. (2) Divvy up *abbrev.* of divide up. To allocate various proportions and share.

dob (in) To inform an authority, often clandestinely, of a perceived wrongdoing. The word is derived from a British dialect expression where dob meant to put an object down heavily. In New Zealand and Australia, the term came to mean passing information behind someone's back, thus betraying them and causing them trouble. Initially some rancour gathered around the figure who had done the dobbing. A gradual change took place, so that 'to dob in' came to mean informing authorities of a hitherto undetected misdemeanour. In 2000 the Auckland Regional Council put into action a campaign called Dob a Smokey, encouraging motorists to phone in the licence plate of any car seen emitting excessive exhaust fumes. This encouragement from the establishment

helped to shift the perception of dobbing towards doing a social good.
(See **pot, to**)

docket A paper referring to a sale, with information about contents, price and delivery instructions, often functioning as receipt or proof of purchase.
(See **bill**)

dodgy (1) Non-standard, of doubtful efficiency or morality. (2) Difficult to achieve without organisational dexterity.

dogbox, in the To be excluded from something, often from a level of personal relationship or professional respect, through having transgressed in some way. The image is related to an earlier American version, doghouse, made popular by a 1954 Dean Martin–Nat King Cole duet, 'Open up the Doghouse, Two Cats are Coming In'. Dogbox also retains its literal meaning in New Zealand.

dog tucker A mess, a failure. Originally the term referred to an old horse or cow with little value but whose meat could feed dogs, who are not noted for their culinary discrimination. By extension it came to mean any project, career or occasion that lacks merit and is destined to degenerate into ineffectiveness, or already has. *The shop started out being profitable, but customers dwindled, the premises began to look run down and the whole business was little better than dog tucker.*

dole A benefit or stipend paid by the government to assist someone unemployed. It is related to an ancient Saxon word, *del*, which described the piece of land given annually to peasant families to work. After Britain introduced an unemployment benefit in 1911 – a portion of financial help to be given to each man who could not find work – it gradually became known as dole. Although the formal and official name for an unemployment benefit is changed from time to time,

New Zealanders still tend to refer to it as the dole. Other countries are more likely to say welfare or relief.

A dole bludger is someone who takes a government benefit without genuinely satisfying the official eligibility criteria.
(See **bludge**)

domain   A park, usually for public use and administered by a public authority.
(See **reserve**)

domes   Stud fasteners, press studs, snap studs.

donny, donnybrook   A brawl, a physical fight, often connected with alcohol. The term is widely used in New Zealand, though its origin is Irish, from a district near Dublin where the annual fair was reputedly known for many outbreaks of spontaneous fisticuffs.

doodackie, **dooflicky** (also **hoodicky**, **hoodackie**) A gimmick, novelty, or a substitute reference for any object whose exact name will not come to mind, or is unknown at the time. The terms are derived from First World War military slang for small detachable fittings.

doozie   Something unique, outstanding, or especially pleasing. The word originates from the English custom of describing something appealing as a 'daisy', a usage which had moved to the United States by the 1840s. During the later part of that century, the fame of the Italian actress Eleanor Duse is believed to have influenced a development from daisy to doozie. A belief that doozie was an abbreviation of the American car the Duesenberg is unfounded, since the word was well established long before the car was ever seen. *I've seen him kick a goal from tricky positions before, but this one was a real doozie!*

double   Way of saying a repeated number. When speaking phone or street numbers which contain a repeated digit, rather than saying 88 or 33 New Zealanders often say double 8 or double 3, as in the universal designation of James Bond – Double-O-7.

double dipping   The practice of drawing two forms of income simultaneously and illicitly, often at least one being from a government source, e.g. a person with a paying job who is also receiving an unemployment benefit.

down the tubes, gurgler, toilet   Ruined, ineffective, at the end of its usefulness. *She put all her savings into buying that boarding house, but then it was condemned by the council, and her investment went down the tubes.*

do your block   To display anger in a definite and noisy way. The expression signifies giving way to the anger in one's head. *When he went to collect the television set, they said the repair wasn't done and he'd have to wait another two days. Boy, did he do his block!*
(See **block, knock someone's block off, use your block**)

drag the chain   Working etc. more slowly than others in a group. The term arose from the image of harnessed animals not pulling at full strength, thus allowing the harness to slacken. It was also influenced by shearers who work in a chain – one slow worker delays the rhythm of the chain. *We want to avoid having Stella on food. She drags the chain, and we won't get enough sandwiches made before lunch.*

drapes   Curtains of solid woven fabric. The term does not usually include thin net window coverings. Developed originally as an upmarket term, drapes originally evoked an image of wide expanses of heavy damask in large mansions, but is now widely used for all kinds of curtains.

dressing gown   A loose-fitting indoors coat, usually buttonless and wraparound with a soft tie-belt, which is worn for modesty or warmth or both, when you are not dressed to be seen publicly. Elsewhere the garment is often known as a bathrobe or just robe.

drongo A person who is very slow-witted. Although there have been various theories, the word's origin is unknown and it may just be that it sounds foolish and funny. There appears to be no connection with the drongo bird from Madagascar, which gives no appearance of being stupid. There is a possible link with a well-known racehorse of that name in Australia during the 1920s which, although a good galloper, always raced disappointingly, but nothing has been proved. *Marie is engaged to that bloke from the insurance firm. What a pair: she's so bright and he's such a drongo.*

drop kick (1) A technique in rugby of dropping the ball and kicking it as it bounces up. (2) A loser, someone whose level of alertness is less than ideal.

dry horrors Unpleasantness during and after an alcoholic hangover. Dealing with recent drunkenness and lacking fluids, those parts of the body lacking sufficient moisture borrow it from other areas. The result is a feeling of great instability, even disorientation, and a need to take in as much fluid as possible.

dub *abbrev*. of double. Fit a second person onto a bike, thus doubling the number it carries.

duck shove Ineffective activity, usually caused by avoidance of decision and passing on responsibility (especially in a context of officialdom and bureaucracy). Ducks do shove each other but New Zealand slang watcher David McGill traces the expression to 19th-century taxi drivers in Melbourne jumping the queue and not parking at the end of the line when they came into a rank.

duff, up the duff (1) Arising from a British dialect pronunciation of dough, duff came to mean a dough-based pudding, usually steamed. When including dried fruits, it is often called plum duff. (2) Up the duff – pregnant. Several centuries ago pudding was a euphemism for penis. Because a real pudding was made from dough, often pronounced duff, an association grew between the concepts and the pregnancy idea developed. Associated terms include in the pudding club and the verb to duff (to make pregnant). Bun in the oven may have arisen by association with duff/pudding, and both expressions are assisted by the physical shape of pregnancy.

dummy   (1) The rubber teat sucked on by babies (sometimes known elsewhere as a pacifier). (2) A ventriloquist's doll, or imitative copy of something real, such as artificial fruit.
(See **spit the dummy**)

dunger   An old piece of machinery, usually a car, which may be still effective and not even feeble, but is noisy. The word is believed to have developed by imitating the sound of a less-than-perfect engine: dung-a-dung-a-dung.

dunny   Informal term for a lavatory. It is possible that the word is derived from an old Scots dialect word *dunnakin*, which originally meant a kind of cellar. There is a strong belief however that, in New Zealand and Australia, dunny has developed separately, based on the facility's inevitable close association with dung.

duvet   A warm lightweight spread on top of a bed. The term is derived from the French word for birds' down. The New Zealand use of the name suggests that the whole spread is filled with down and soft feathers, though this is not always the case. The French call the same thing a couette and there are other English names: eiderdown, continental quilt, comforter, puff. In Australia the same object is customarily known as a doona, which is a trade name based on a Scandinavian word for down.

dux The title given to the top academic student for the year in a New Zealand school. It comes from the Latin for leader, which also developed into duke. The United States has a valedictorian.

dwang A piece of timber secured horizontally between upright studs, to strengthen a wall frame. This is also sometimes called a noggin or nog, which was originally a small brick-shaped piece of timber placed in a brick wall at a point where a nail would need to be hammered in. When timber houses became more common, similar small wooden pieces were needed between studs on a weight-bearing wall and they, too, came to be called nogs. Dwang is derived from a Dutch word signifying strength, and in Britain its meaning is entirely different: in many areas of British industry, such as the Mersey shipyards, a dwang is a strong wrench used for turning taps and reamers.

E

easy as pie Very simple to accomplish. The term has been used familiarly in New Zealand since the early 1920s but its derivation is not clear. Two explanations have been presented: (1) An old English alphabet mnemonic starts 'a is for apple-pie' and once a small child had mastered this, it would doubtless seem easy. (2) A more widely believed theory is that the expression is a rare example of bilingualism, pai being the Maori word for good, agreeable. Thus, saying that something was 'easy and pai' indicated that it was both not difficult and pleasurable. Combinations of Maori and English are rare. Both possible explanations of the expression's origin seem to overlook the fact that making an actual pie isn't necessarily easy.
(See **kapai, half-pie**)

eh A speech particle with several purposes. (1) Added to a statement to intensify what has been said, and make it more definite: *I've had a bad day, eh.* (2) Conversely, to transform the statement into an interrogative: *The bus leaves at six o'clock, eh?* (3) Added to a statement in the expectation of agreement from the listener: *That's a beautiful yacht, eh?* (4) An informal way of asking for a statement to be repeated or explained, replacing 'I beg your pardon?': *He plays petanque. Eh?*

The differences are usually discernible by paralanguage – the tone of voice in which the particle is said. The usage of eh is particularly high among Maori speaking English and the derivation is possibly from the Maori 'ne', meaning 'isn't that so'.

e hoa *Maori* A friendly form of address, indicating friend. It is not confined to Maori conversation: it is occasionally used by English speakers as an amiable greeting, especially to someone whose name is not known.

electric jug, hot water jug A metal, ceramic or heavy plastic jug with an electric element inside, which heats water to boiling for such domestic requirements as making tea or coffee. In Britain it is commonly called an electric kettle, or just kettle, and similar abbreviation occurs in New Zealand: it is referred to simply as the jug. In most parts of the United States, this appliance and its name are virtually unknown.

electric puha Slang term for marijuana. Puha is a thistle weed much prized in Maori cooking, but lacks the electric quality which the leaves of *Cannabis sativa* provide.

End of the Golden Weather The title of a famous New Zealand one-man show, portraying 40 characters, written and performed, for 19 years, by the late Dr Bruce Mason, a prolific writer of radio talks, short stories and plays. Drawn largely from his own childhood memories, *The End of the Golden Weather* was first performed in 1959. It was later made into a TV special and rewritten as a full-cast play, then made into a full-length movie. The title is a quote from a 1941 American novel by Thomas Clayton Wolfe, *The Web and the Rock*. The expression has gone into popular usage in New Zealand to indicate that a period of something pleasurable is coming to, or has come to, an end.

engaged (tone, signal) The sound indicating that an attempted phone call cannot be connected because the person being called is already on the phone. New Zealanders say the phone, or the person, is engaged; the word 'busy' is more common overseas.

en suite Bathroom and toilet opening directly off a bedroom and intended only for the use of that room's occupants. The term is derived from the French for 'in sequence' or 'following'. When American accommodation has something similar it is often called a half bath.

entrée The opening part of the meal, an appetiser or starter. From the French word for an opening or introduction, entrée is used by some other cultures to refer to the main course itself.
(See **main**)

Erewhon The fictional name, an anagram of 'nowhere', inspired by the high-country sheep farm in Canterbury called Mesopotamia Station. Samuel Butler wrote the satirical novel *Erewhon* in 1871, when he was back in England after living and working in New Zealand between 1860 and 1864. The novel is widely believed to be based on his experiences on his land at Mesopotamia.

eskimo pie A small oblong of ice cream coated with chocolate. It is a trade name, patented by the firm of Stover Confectionery, Chicago, in 1922.

eyes out Proceeding at full tilt, with full energy, as strongly as possible. This term, which arose in New Zealand and Australia in the 1860s, is of unknown origin, but appears only to refer to the physical state of extreme exertion when the eyes appear to become wider.

F

fa'afafine *Samoan* (pronounced fah-ah-fah-fee-nay). The term, which accurately means 'like a woman', describes a not uncommon phenomenon in Samoan society, where some males grow their hair long, wear female cosmetics and clothes and undertake duties traditionally assigned to women in the community. The lifestyle has been completely accepted within Samoa for many centuries and is not equivalent to the European drag queen. Non-Samoans, who have difficulty with the glottal stop, customarily leave it out and pronounce the term as fah-fah-fee-nay.

fagged out Tired, exhausted. The term originates with the word flag – in its sense of being worn out and drooping. Thus the errand boy in a British school (the fag) has his normal work plus errands for the senior, so he is overworked and flagged or fagged. And a handmade cigarette hanging from someone's lips can look droopy and flagged, so it too became a fag.

fair dinkum Intensifiers such as real and square were originally added to dinkum to signify absolute honesty, but fair is now the most common intensifier. The phrase is also used interrogatively, seeking reassurance that what you have just been told can be verified by further assurance.
(See **dinkum**)

fair go An honest deal, with equitable treatment. When said alone, it can also be a statement of surprise or mild interrogation: *Fair go? Do you really mean that?* Although related to the British expressions fair deal and fair do's, the New Zealand version comes from the game of two-up, where the call 'fair go' indicates that the game is all set up and ready to go. A New Zealand television programme entitled *Fair Go*, which tackles consumer complaints in a popular and palatable style, began in 1977 and is still screening. The programme's slogan is: 'If you've been ripped off, short-changed or given the runaround, and nobody wants to know – we do!'

fantail   A small native bird with a perfect fan-shaped tail. *Rhipidura fuliginosa* in Latin or piwakawaka (tiwakawaka) in Maori, the fantail is characterised by its cheeky and charming behaviour, rapid darting flight movements and high chirps and twitterings.
(See **piwakawaka, tiwakawaka**)

farmstay   A short-term stay on a rural property which takes in paying guests.

fibrolite   An exterior wallboard made originally from a kind of asbestos, compressed and moulded into flat sheets. Fibrolite is a trade name, registered in 1916 by James Hardie & Co.

fit as a buck rat   Ready for action and very healthy. Similar to fit as a fiddle but with a rather more typically New Zealand physical slant.

fizz boat   Any small motor-driven craft. Thought to be so named because of its seemingly rapid motion and the fizzy water disturbance its progress causes.

flake out, flakers   (1) Exhausted. (2) Depending on context, drunk, hungover. (3) Faint. Thought originally to be used at sea, when a person became unconscious, either deeply asleep or drunk, the term grew into general acceptance in New Zealand and Australia, as flakers or flaked out, with a similar meaning, though in a sympathetic rather than pejorative sense.

flannel, flannel leaf   (1) A small washcloth used to apply soapy water, sometimes just to the face. It is customarily made of heavy cotton weave, rather than flannel. (2) Flannel leaf – a tall bush-shaped weed (*Solanum mauritianum*) native to Uruguay which has become a noxious weed in New Zealand, sometimes growing to 10 metres tall. It is forbidden from sale and must be exterminated by householders when observed. Also known as woolly nightshade and (informally) as bushman's friend because the large soft flexible leaves form an effective substitute for toilet paper. A similar plant in Britain is known as mullen or mullein.

flat A set of rooms within a larger building, functioning as a separate residence. The name dates back to the word's meaning of horizontal. Originally a flat was a set of rooms within a larger building, all on one level – hence the description flat. In spite of changing architectural patterns, by which gradually flats did begin to include staircases, and the American preference for the word apartment, in New Zealand the word flat remains in common use. Parallel developments include to flat and flatting, and flatters or flatmates. (In the United States, a flat means only a punctured tyre – which has thus become horizontal!)

flat stick, flat to the boards, flat tack Travelling as fast as possible and making the maximum effort. These popular New Zealand expressions are probably derived from a combination of images concerning speed: (1) a car accelerator pushed hard, thus flat and parallel to the floor of the vehicle, (2) a pilot's use of a stick when flying, and (3) from horse-riding, when the whip is in a horizontal position as the horse is being urged to go faster. The origin of flat tack is even less clear: it possibly refers to the fact that when a tack has been hammered in as far as it will go, it is flat. *If we work flat stick we'll get all this fruit picked by tonight.*

flattie (1) Shoes with a low heel, or none. (2) A punctured tyre. (3) *abbrev.* of New Zealand flatfish (aka flounder, sole, brill).

flax A tall native plant with long strap-like leaves of a rigid format, growing in lowland swamps and alluvial soils. The richly fibrous leaves have been and still are widely used by Maori, who call the plant harakeke, to make carrying kits, skirts, cloaks, fishing nets and ropes. The flowers yield nectar which attracts many birds. The common name flax derives from an error made in 1770 when Captain Cook's scientists decided it was related to European flax. In fact New Zealand flax could more correctly be called hemp and has no connection with European flax (*Linum usitatissimum*), whose fibre comes from its stalks, not leaves. In 1772 the New Zealand plant was officially named *Phormium tenax*, based on the Latin for strong baskets.

In pre-European times, Maori were so skilled with the plant that an industry developed, making expertly dressed flax fibres into rigging ropes for sailing ships, and general rope-making. By 1873 there were 300 New Zealand flax mills in operation. The industry waxed and waned according to world events, such as the American Civil War and the First World War, but the decline of sailing ships and the invention of synthetic fibres caused production to decline.

But useful though it still is, New Zealand flax plays no part in the production of fine high-fashion linens which, according to international label laws, must be made from fibres of European flax.

fly cemeteries Popular soft biscuit-like delicacies, formally known as fruit squares, with two slim layers of pastry or cake containing a compressed dried-fruit mixture with a large proportion of raisins and currants. During cooking the fruit mixture becomes a glossy black colour and develops a chewy toffee-like texture. Early in the 20th century a British wit coined the name fly cemeteries for currant-pudding and currant-cakes and New Zealanders applied the term to fruit squares because the central fruit layer resembled a collection of squashed dead flies.

flying fox An arrangement of ropes connected to pulleys and a small platform that allows a person or goods to cross water or a gully when no conventional bridge is available. The name comes from the Pacific Island fruit bat which, in spite of its comparatively large size and furry appearance, can fly and float quite easily.

FOB *abbrev.* of fresh off the boat (pronounced as fob). Pacific Island immigrants who have recently come to live in New Zealand. Originally pejorative, the term was later adopted by Pacific Islanders themselves and used positively, even, in recent years, as the name of a play and a concert. A contracted form is sometimes used: freshies.

fonged Drunk. The word is based on an older use of fong referring, inexplicably, to methylated spirits, which the desperate have been known to buy and sip.

foodie Someone with a deep interest in all aspects of food: its qualities, social values and origins, the finer details of its preparation, taste, texture and presentation.

forest Seldom used colloquially of large treed areas, which are called bush, forest occurs in formal contexts, e.g. state forest (a treed area under government supervision), and when referring to areas that have been deliberately planted in exotic trees. (See **bush**)

free-to-air Electronic transmission, usually television, which is available to the general public without charge (as opposed to pay, cable and satellite TV).

freezing works Abattoir where beasts are killed for their meat and hides.

fringe Hair styled to leave one section hanging over the forehead. Elsewhere a fringe is sometimes called bangs.

full on Extended to the limit, intense. Although frequently used in a metaphorical rather than a literal sense, it still evokes the image of a horse galloping as fast as it can, or an engine with open throttle.

funny as a fit Something very amusing. This is the New Zealand equivalent of funny as a fight, although both comparisons are illogical.

G

galoot An awkward or clumsy person. The word became established in English in the early 1800s and is used freely in New Zealand but not commonly in other countries. The word's origin is believed to be nautical, based on the Russian *golut*, slave, and originally used in referring to unsure young seamen.

gap your axe Indicating annoyance though malfunction. The term, which probably began with woodsmen and foresters, is usually heard as Wouldn't that gap your axe?, meaning Wouldn't that annoy you? The expression has a literal basis: the efficiency of an axe blade is ruined if it is accidentally struck and notched. Known since at least the 1930s, the phrase was also used in the shearing sheds: Wouldn't that gap your shears?

garage sale A popular suburban practice whereby household goods are sold in and around an emptied domestic garage, usually at a weekend. The event is customarily advertised by home-made signs pinned to power poles around the nearby streets and outside the house holding the sale.
(See **boot sale**)

gawk (1) A person perceived as stupid, mainly because of their awkward movement. (2) To stare at in a fixed manner. There is an occasional interaction with gawp, also meaning a stupid stare. Gawk, which is believed to originate in a Danish word *gaukr* (related to gape), is heard more in New Zealand than elsewhere, though it is used in Yorkshire meaning left-handed, which is often perceived as awkward.

Gecko A type of small New Zealand native lizard (*Gekkonidae*).

geek, gink, gekko (sometimes **dekko**), **gander** A brief look with a particular intent, rather than a general survey. The words may all be variations on the early use of gander, an 1880s British dialect term meaning a look, based on the image of a gander as a long-necked bird who seems to peer at things.

Gentle Annie The name of several places in New Zealand – hills and gorges, a bridge, a bay and a hill track. It is thought to come from an old Stephen Foster song: ' When the springtime comes, gentle Annie, and the wildflowers are scattered o'er the plain'. There is also the story about a 19th-century New Zealand barmaid who made such an impact on the local miners that she was remembered in place names. Gentle Annie reappeared in late 20th-century New Zealand as the brand name for a washing machine and as the title of a country music group.
(See **Roaring Meg**)

geoduck The world's largest burrowing saltwater clam. The New Zealand variety (*Panopea zelandica*) can grow to 1 kilogram or more in weight, and other related species on the coasts of Japan, the United States and Canada can be larger. The most noticeable characteristic of the shellfish is its thick meaty protruding siphon which, in some species, grows to 1 metre. The name has nothing to do with ducks: it is believed to be based on a native American word meaning dig deep. In a prime example of metathesis – reversal of a word's middle syllables – geoduck is normally pronounced gooey-duck.

get in behind A command given to (usually rural) dogs to come to heel. This broadened into a gentle and semi-humorous way of telling someone to behave properly. There are two other extensions of meaning: (1) to signify that a person or group is going to support a proposal (get in behind it), and (2) as an ejaculation of surprise or disbelief: *You're running for Parliament? Get in behind!*)

get off the grass An exclamation expressing either (1) disdain concerning the opinion offered, or (2) disbelief that what has been said could possibly be true.

get on it Euphemism for an intake of alcohol, either singly or as a group, and often at the exclusion of such associated activities as dining. The drinking becomes an end in itself.

get the wind up To become nervous or afraid. Arising from the British armed services during the First World War, the expression is believed to be based on a parody version of the song 'British Grenadiers', to which troops sang ribald new words, including a reference to the Battle of Waterloo, at which the wind blew up someone's trousers, 'and he didn't know what to do'. In New Zealand it is often contracted to windy.

gidday, g'day *abbrev.* of *good day*. This has been in print in New Zealand since 1919 as an informal greeting, usually reproducing identifiably working class usage, but by 2000 the term had become an ordinary greeting, though perhaps still said slightly jokingly by the educated.

give it a go To attempt, to try. The expression is often used in a context where it implies a certain amount of boldness or courage. An early New Zealand television show for children was entitled *Gizago*, which contemporary newspapers found it necessary to translate as 'let me have a try'.

give it heaps To make a great effort, to ensure generous energy, to praise unstintingly. Although the following 'of' has disappeared, it is always clear from the context. The expression dates from the early 1980s.
(See **heaps**)

giving me gyp To receive an annoying little irritation, sometimes physical, sometimes circumstantial. Gyp is a contraction of gee-up, as in kick-starting a stubborn horse.

give way An instruction, usually signposted, to drivers to allow oncoming traffic through first. Other countries sometimes use 'yield'.

Gladwrap Micro-thin transparent plastic sheeting, usually used for kitchen purposes. It is known elsewhere as cling-film or handi-wrap.

glide time A supposedly user-friendly work scheme that allows workers to adjust their 40-hour week into personally suitable blocks of time. The concept was initiated by government departments during the 1970s but the main impact on the public in general was via the title of a very funny play (and ensuing TV series called *Gliding On*) by Roger Hall.

glory box The clothes and domestic accoutrements collected by young women in preparation for marriage, and also the receptacle into which they are put. It is also known sometimes as a hope chest. The custom is now seldom observed.

go bush (1) To eschew urban life altogether and live by choice in a rural area without the usual modern conveniences. (2) To hide deliberately, as from authorities such as the police. An adaptation of the early British expression take to the woods, go bush has developed its meaning to also describe someone who cannot be found, even in a big city.
(See **bush**)

Godzone *abbrev.* of God's Own Country. In the New Zealand context, the expression dates from a phrase in Thomas Bracken's very long 1893 poem written in praise of New Zealand. Premier Dick Seddon boosted the phrase's popularity. In 1906, on his way home from Australia, Seddon sent a telegram to New Zealand saying that he was returning to 'God's Own Country'. He died the next day, but the expression outlived him and, thanks to eminent poet Allen Curnow, changed slightly to Godzone. God's Own Country has also been used in connection with India, Rhodesia (now Zimbabwe), the United States and Australia.

going crook See **crook**

going nuts (1) Slang for mentally unbalanced. (2) Becoming angry. (3) As just nuts – exclamation of irritable disbelief.

gone to the dogs Deterioration of performance and efficiency in a person or system, akin to gone to pieces. The image comes from the medieval habit of throwing leftovers of food to the dogs; the scraps were of no further use to the diners, hence the image of uselessness. *That shop used to stock really high-class goods but now it's gone to the dogs.*

gone to the pack Losing a position of control or supremacy, slipping to a mundane and lower level of life. The image comes from that of a dog leading a wild pack, who falls from prominence and becomes just one of the group. *Brett just went to the pack after the divorce.*

good as gold Expression of goodwill and approval; everything is agreed and will proceed. The expression has been used in Britain since the 17th century, but usually only in reference to a child's manners and behaviour.

good keen man (sometimes **bloke**) A reliable person, exhibiting the best of qualities associated with the New Zealand male. A rural government official used the term in a letter, describing the young Barry Crump, then a deerstalker, as a good keen man. The phrase was later used as the title of Crump's first book, published in 1960. Following its success, Crump became an extremely popular author, specialising in adventures in a rural context, and written in strictly New Zealand vernacular.

good oh (sometimes **o**) Expression of agreement or approval.

good on you, good for you Expressions of approval and encouragement.

go on Expression of mild disbelief when being told something of very doubtful truth. *I've been told I have the potential to be a high-fashion model.' 'Go on.'*

go to whoa From start to stop, from beginning to end. In this form the expression has been a familiar one in New Zealand since the 1950s. The reverse – whoa to go, meaning from stop to start – is often used by car enthusiasts to describe how long it takes for a stationary vehicle to get up to full speed. In New Zealand whoa, the command used to halt a horse, is generally pronounced 'woo', but in these expressions the pronunciation changes back to the rhyming 'wo'.

graft (sometimes **hard graft**) Hard work. The word originated in Britain, where in old dialect it signified digging. The word is used as both a noun and a verb. *Sean clawed his way to the top by sheer hard graft.*

greaser (1) An unexpected and ungraceful fall. It is sometimes used as a metaphor when, for example, a business or a career or a relationship has come a greaser. (2) A toady, a person who makes themselves friendly or overhelpful to gain advantage. They are said to have greased up to the boss, an elderly relation, the neighbour's wife, etc.

greasies Food, especially takeaway food, quickly cooked in fat.

greenstone Semi-precious nephrite and bowenite stone, also known as New Zealand jade (though it is not strictly jade). Its beautiful green colour makes it attractive for creating jewellery, but because the stone is also hard and durable, Maori used pounamu, as they called it, to make adzes, chisels and fighting clubs. In English it began as green stone in 1769, by 1817 had become green-stone and in 1864 appeared as one word, greenstone.

Jade from other countries is often made into ornaments and sold as 'greenstone', but commercial and souvenir outlets in New Zealand deliberately use the word pounamu (rather than greenstone) to make clear that items so labelled are of genuinely New Zealand origin.

grocer A dealer in foodstuffs and household supplies, operating out of a shop called a grocery. The word, which comes from the old French word *gross*, meaning large amounts, has all but vanished from the New Zealand vocabulary since the dominance of supermarkets.

grog-on (also **grogging on** and **grog on regardless**). Continuing an extended session of social drinking. Similar to **on the grog** – enjoyment of alcohol, usually in a celebratory context.

ground floor The ground level floor of any multi-storey building. The next floor up is the 'first' floor. This is very confusing for American visitors who call the ground floor the first floor and think that the 'G' on the board in a lift stands for garage.

grouse (1) Excellent, approved, attractive. Any object, person, project or idea that meets the listener's standards of pleasure, can be grouse. The term is often used by men about a woman who appeals, either for her looks or other qualities. (2) To complain, grumble and whinge.

grundies, grunds Informal colloquial term for men's underwear. The derivation is thought to be a rhyme with undies.

grunt Power, strength, in the abstract or the positive. It can be used of a car, an individual's influence or even the amount of garlic in a spaghetti bolognaise. It is often used in the phrase 'a ton of grunt'.

Guard Pacific's triple star Nobody has any definite explanation of the exact meaning of this obscure line in New Zealand's national anthem, written by Thomas Bracken.

These are the main theories:

(1) New Zealand used to be divided into three provinces – New Ulster, New Munster and New Leinster – but these had been disestablished more than 20 years before the song was written.

(2) New Zealand's three main islands: North, South and Stewart. But there are many more islands than that.

(3) Real stars in the sky? But the Southern Cross, which appears on New Zealand's flag, has four.

(4) Bracken really meant truple, an abbreviated form of quadruple. No, he definitely wrote triple.

(5) It was a misprint: Bracken actually wrote 'triple shore'. Bracken supervised the printing through several stages and it always said star. And what would triple shore mean anyway?

(6) Perhaps he was referring to a flag: the Union Jack has three crosses on it and the Paerangi flag, associated with the Maori King movement since 1857, includes three actual stars. Was Bracken, in 1876, familiar with these?

(7) Bishop Selwyn's coat of arms features three stars. Would Catholic Bracken, down in Dunedin, have revered or even known about the insignia of an Anglican bishop in far-off Northland?

Conclusion: Nobody knows what 'triple star' actually means.

gully A small valley, ravine, gorge, eroded watercourse, or depression on a flat. The word, which comes from the Latin *gula* meaning throat (which also survives in gullet), was used by Captain Cook to describe the ravines eroded by water courses he saw in New Zealand.

gumboots Rubber or plastic waterproof boots. Various versions reach either to ankle, knee or thigh. The British, who call their gumboots wellingtons or wellies, favour green but New Zealand gumboots (gummies) are customarily black – carbon added to the rubber makes it black and makes the rubber more durable. The central North Island rural town of Taihape promotes itself as the 'Gumboot Capital of New Zealand'. It boasts a giant corrugated iron sculpture of a gumboot and holds a nationally known annual gumboot-throwing contest in which participants endeavour to toss a gumboot the greatest distance across a paddock.

gun   See **big gun**

gurgler   See **down the tubes**

gutser   An awkward fall (often used metaphorically). The word originally referred to that kind of an accidental fall in which someone landed flat on their stomach, and so 'came a gutser'. Any noticeably significant failure of, say, a business or a project, can be said to have come a gutser.

gyp   See **giving me gyp**

H

had it At the end of one's tether, exhausted or exasperated, a lost chance. It is usually used in a phrase such as 'I've had it' but can also be an adjective, as in 'a had it engine'. Very common, too, is 'I've had it up to here', occasionally with a gesture to the neck, to indicate that someone is completely fed up.

haere mai *Maori* Welcome. It is also used to mean come here, come to me, as when addressed to a child or family pet, when food is ready.

haere ra *Maori* Farewell, but rather more formal and graceful than just goodbye. There is no foundation for an early belief that haere ra was a transliteration of the informal New Zealand way of saying goodbye: hooray.

haggle Usually signifies persistent bargaining. A particular New Zealand use has arisen, referring to a bet made between players on a golf course, sometimes devised to allow varying payouts for every player. The percentage varies according to scores but all the funds come from the losing team.

haka *Maori* A shouting dance of strength, a posture dance, usually (but not always) performed by men. There are hundreds of types of haka. They are not, as is often supposed, only war dances or challenges to supremacy, as on the sports field. In any genuinely aggressive situation, such as war, the Maori haka has definitely meant business and could freeze the blood of any enemy, but a haka can be part of a welcome, an affirmation of loyalty or a gesture of farewell (as when members of 28 Maori Battalion left their communities in the Second World War). The key words are strength and passion, according to the particular sentiment being expressed.
(See **Ka mate, ka mate**)

half cut Drunk. One of the many meanings of cut is finished, often applied to a source of food or more especially alcohol. A barrel of beer that is cut has been drained dry, but when its consumers are half cut they will be well past being sober.

half-hitch To steal. Although the term appears to be connected more with a kind of knot than with illegal possession, it is believed to be an obscure form of rhyming slang – the rhyme for half-hitch being snitch (steal), or possibly a play on another stealing-word, pinch, and its rhyme, half-inch, which developed into half-hitch.

half-pie Not commendably good or properly done. This common New Zealand expression is a rare linguistic combination – an English word placed with a Maori word (pai, meaning good, fine, commendable), each retaining their original meaning but combining to form a new word with a third meaning.
(See **kapai, easy as pie**)

handle A glass mug with a handle, for drinking beer. Many ceramic mugs and steins for beer-drinkers also have handles, but beer-glasses for the dining table customarily do not. Glass drinking vessels with handles seems to fit with the laid-back ambience of a pub, rather than the restraint of a restaurant. A handle can also mean the amount of beer within the glass mug.

hangi *Maori* Food cooked underground, usually in sufficient quantity to feed a number of people. A deep hole is dug, and its base lined with very hot (and heat-retaining) stones. Wrapped bundles of food are placed on the stones, the bundles are covered with mats and then the mats are covered with earth and the hole totally filled. The captured heat and steam cooks the food, deliciously. Putting down a hangi is usually a happy, communal occasion. The word umu *(Maori* and *Samoan)* is also sometimes used for a hangi.

hang of a A qualifier or intensifier that increases what it is applied to. The term seems to have arisen on both sides of the Tasman as a genteel version of 'a hell of a', with 'a heck of a' along the way. A lot of mud on the rugby field is not as much as a heck of a lot. A harvest is obviously a lavish one if a hang of a lot of grapes are picked.

hapu *Maori* There are two meanings. (1) The wider and more general meaning is 'extended family': parents and grandparents, the sisters and brothers of those grandparents, and the children and grandchildren of the aunts, uncles and great-aunts and great-uncles. Sometimes hapu can be used to refer to your sub-tribe. (2) Pronounced in a slightly different way, hapu also means pregnant.

hapuku *Maori* A large fish, a species of sea bass, *Polyprion oxygeneios*, which provides excellent food. Since it first came to the attention of early European settlers, the Maori name has had nearly 20 different spellings. Hapuku comes closest to being accurate, though the mis-spelling hapuka is common.

hard case A daredevil, probably quick on the uptake, capable of giving amusement and shrewd without being dishonest. The term originated in Britain, meaning a tough fellow, known for courage and lack of fear. The term was used in that way in New Zealand until the early 1900s; by 1914 the term had become complimentary.
(Note: not to be confused with head case, which means a crazy and unbalanced person.)

hard word Persistent persuasion to agree to a proposition. The term can apply to involvement in any activity or project but is most often applied when seeking sex. Far from pleading or importuning, the expression conveys confidence by depicting the outcome as inevitable acquiescence.

hard yakka Work that is demanding, rather than leisurely. An adaptation of an Aboriginal dialect word *yaga*, meaning work, yakka was adopted by European immigrants to Australia as a slang term, and has been used since the 1850s. Adding 'hard' reinforces the point. (The term can also occasionally be heard referring to cerebral work, such as concentrated preparation for an examination.)

hash-house A restaurant or café that serves indifferent food. Generally the various meanings of hash are associated with something being chopped into small pieces. The term is also found in Hash House Harriers, an informal title for groups of people who go running as a social activity. The association between hash house and harriers began with British civil servants in Singapore, who were less than enchanted with the unimaginative meals supplied by the Selangor Club, which they called 'the hash house'. In 1938 their social running club borrowed the name.

haurangi *Maori* Drunk or, depending on context, crazy.

Hawaiki The original homeland for all Polynesian peoples. It is frequently referred to in legend, but has never been exactly identified geographically. The word was first used in written English by Joseph Banks in 1770.

he, I'll go The focus position (he) in children's games such as hide'n'seek, when whoever is he closes eyes while the group hides. By extension, the term can also apply in any situation where a leader is required, hence the offer, I'll go he.

head sherang The chief executive, the boss. The word came into English from an Urdu word *serang*, meaning the principal authority, especially of a ship. (Many British merchant vessels had Urdu-speaking Indian crews.) It can be pronounced with just an *s* sound at the beginning, but most New Zealanders say sherang. The addition of head is a tautology.

heaps A large amount, either literally or, more usually,

figuratively. The word is very often used with ellipsis, omitting the following 'of' because the heaps do not need to be specifically identified. *My partner made me late for the airport, so I gave him heaps.*
(See **give it heaps**)

herringbone shed A cowshed in which the bails are positioned in a row all at the same angle, with a facing row angled in the opposite direction. Someone noticed the layout's similarity to the backbone of a herring and by 1959 this became the accepted name.

hiding Informal word either for a literal thrashing or, metaphorically, for an ignominious defeat in some kind of contest. The origin appears to be an old English reference to being beaten on the hide. The word is used even when no body contact is involved: the loser is given a hiding. 'Good hiding' is also common, indicating greater intensity.
(See **thrashing**)

hiding to nothing A certainty of failure, despite a lot of effort. For instance, a sports team facing a match it cannot win might say, 'We're on a hiding to nothing' even before the game starts.

hikoi *Maori* The act of walking alongside others in a respectful relationship, taking the same journey in the same direction. The term came to prominent public attention in 1975 when Dame Whina Cooper led a hikoi on foot from the top of the North Island to Wellington, as a non-violent protest against the validity of some Crown ownership of formerly Maori lands.

hipi iti *Maori* The meaning is little sheep, but the term has reached prominence as a registered proprietary brand name for a marinated feta cheese made from ewes' milk.

hissy fit A solo explosion of unease, or an argument between two or more people. Probably not of New Zealand origin, the image is undoubtedly based on two cantankerous cats. In its New Zealand use, the term suggests a silly fuss.

hoe into Devoting oneself to a task with notable energy, enthusiasm and even sometimes aggression. The term can be applied equally to wolfing food or physically fighting – either initiating it, or responding to provocation. As a metaphor the term is also commonly applied to non-physical applications, such as determinedly studying towards a certificate, or working in a cerebral occupation such as law. The image arises directly from the vigour needed to use a garden hoe effectively, and is synonymous with the expression 'to get stuck into'.

hogget A young sheep when it loses its two centre front milk teeth (and therefore stops being a lamb) at approximately one year old. From then on, but only for the next 12 months, it is referred to as a two-tooth or hogget. In terms of sheep meat, the youngest variety is lamb (up to approximately one year old), followed by hogget (the meat is never referred to as two-tooth, only the animal itself) and from then on, mutton.

hoha *Maori* A person who is useless – apathetic, uninterested, lazy, and causing exasperation and irritation. In reverse, a person can come to be hoha through frustration at bureaucratic delays or the behaviour of those with whom they feel out of kilter.

hokey-pokey Ice cream containing scattered pieces of caramelised sugar which have little bubbles created by the addition of soda. In other countries a similar caramelised sugar confection is called honeycomb, humbug, butter brittle or seafoam candy, though none of these is exactly like the New Zealand version. First sold in New Zealand during the 1940s, hokey-pokey ice cream has been part of the New Zealand dietary landscape since the 1950s. No one knows the origin of the name hokey-pokey.

hoki *Maori* A fish (*Macruronus novaezelandiae*) widely considered one of the most important commercial species. It is usually taken by middle-water trawling and the yearly amount is controlled by a quota system. Sometimes referred to as blue hake, blue grenadier, whiptail or whiting (the latter being a mistake – hoki is not a whiting).

holding A brief and informal way of saying that a person has cash available. *Justin can buy the movie tickets – he's holding. I'm not.*

Hollywood, do a Any form of showing distress, either physical or mental, that is perceived as possibly not genuine. The term is sometimes applied to sports participants who exaggerate a minor injury. It is also used to describe someone vehemently declaring their innocence in a courtroom. *He tripped on the bottom step and fell over, then got up making loud groaning noises and limping. I think he was doing a Hollywood, because he didn't want to go to the dance that night.*

home and dried, home and hosed Both expressions convey the euphoria of success, and can be used to refer to a win that has already happened, or as a prediction of a certain win. In its most literal form, the expression appears to have developed from the standard horse-racing practice in which, after training sessions and after races, horses are taken home and hosed.

There are two other, less popular theories. (1) Because hosed is sometimes the way beer is poured, someone was home and hosed when a job was done and it was time for a drink. (2) In sailing terms, an anchor when lifted back onto the ship (home) is hosed down.

honesty box A simple box, usually wooden, with a slot through which a customer can slide money. An honesty box is often used where there is no supervision of payment for goods on sale – for instance at a rural roadside stall selling fruit and vegetables, or in a communal waiting room or staffroom, where people can make their own tea or coffee and take biscuits from a jar, but are expected to put the equivalent cash in the box provided.

hongi *Maori* A Maori form of greeting where noses are pressed together and the position momentarily held, then broken briefly, and repeated. The lips do not touch. Maori have long held that the breath of a person's body is vital to the person concerned, and sharing it with someone is a form of peaceful acknowledgement. Because the hongi is likely to be a unique experience for overseas visitors being greeted by Maori, a discreet explanation beforehand is usually offered.

hoodackie, hooflickie A nonsense name for something whose actual name is unknown, difficult to pronounce or forgotten at the moment of speaking.
(See **doodackie**)

hoo-ha A nonsense word meaning a commotion or fuss. Despite its sound, it has no connection with any Maori word.

hooker A player in the front row of a rugby scrum. The word can be heard frequently in New Zealand, where rugby is enormously popular. Confusion can arise for visitors from countries where hooker means a prostitute.

hoon A lout, an exhibitionist. Before 1939 hoon meant much what it does now – a loutish exhibitionist, usually male. But the word's meaning changed during the Second World War: non-religious conscientious objectors were known to the military as hoons. After 1945 hoon reverted to its original meaning. Also heard are hoonish, hoonism, hooning, hoondom, hoon around, hoon it up, a bit of a hoon, hoon-chaser (traffic police) and hoon-bin (place where drunken sports spectators are put to cool off).

hooray (1) Exclamation of joy, pleasure and celebration, a variant on the British hurrah. New Zealanders have never favoured saying hurrah although it is a common exclamation in Britain. (2) The New Zealand hooray, besides being different in pronunciation from its British equivalent, has developed an extra meaning. It has also come to be an informal version of goodbye. This confuses some British visitors to New Zealand who, when bid hooray, think that their departure is being celebrated! There is no foundation for an early belief that hooray is an Anglicised version of the Maori phrase haere ra. Hooray is hurrah pronounced in a New Zealand fashion.

Hori *Maori* A transliteration of George (the Maori language has no G). Soon after Europeans arrived in New Zealand, Maori, always very much attuned to interesting verbal effects, became intrigued with the names of their new neighbours and often honoured those they admired by adopting their names, in a more mellifluous Maori version, as with the name Henare for Henry. Hori/George became such a frequent and familiar name for Maori men that during the 19th century the word was frequently used for any unknown Maori. He became Hori or a Hori. The word is now regarded as offensive.

hosed off Very displeased. Used since at least the 1950s, the term is usually thought to reflect how anyone would feel if a hose of water were turned on them. Equally common in New Zealand is the stronger 'pissed off', though 'hosed off' would be preferred in polite company.

hospital pass A rugby pass made in dangerous proximity to a defender, or worse, defenders, so the person who now has the ball will immediately be tackled and can, quite literally, finish up in hospital. The player to whom the ball was passed may have one brief moment of glory, and then wake up with concussion and three broken ribs. It is also sometimes known as a Hail Mary pass, because when the ball is passed to a then-vulnerable player, a quick prayer is necessary. The term can be used away from the sports field to describe something that appears advantageous but has a sting in the tail. *Gregor Abernethy has been raised to the rank of ambassador, but it's a hospital pass – his first posting is to Mongolia.*

housie Sometimes given its full title, housie-housie. The term describes a game similar to bingo.

how are you? A rhetorical and ritual question in New Zealand, usually answered by 'Fine, thanks'. No real answer about the state of someone's health is expected or required.

How ya goin'? How's it going? How's tricks? Abbreviations or substitutes for the conventional ritual greeting, How are you? An equally ritual informal reply is usual, along the lines of 'Fine', 'Great', 'Can't complain'.

hua, hooa, ho *Maori* Variants on whore. The pronunciation hooa arose in Britain during the 18th century as an acceptable and polite way of saying whore. That pronunciation came to New Zealand with colonists, and those unfamiliar with it mistakenly thought it to be a Maori word – hence the occasional printing as hua. The young generation of the 21st century adopted a slang variation, ho, as referring to a woman disapproved of, but not necessarily an actual whore.

huhu (grub) *Maori* The plump wriggling caterpillar-like larva of the beetle *Prionoplus reticularis*, also known as huhu in its adult flying stage. The grub is commonly found in decaying vegetation and wood, and in spite of a somewhat unattractive appearance, can be eaten as a delicacy; the taste is said to resemble peanut butter.

hui *Maori* A meeting with a purpose, usually discussion concerning a project, policy, business tactic or a religious matter. It may possibly be more social, such as a big reunion of family members, but the point is that a hui is always a meeting with a focus – an assembly. A hui is usually held on a marae, where certain behaviour and formalities are adhered to. Hui are usually all-Maori affairs, but when both Maori and non-Maori attend, Maori protocols prevail.

huia *Maori* (Latin: *Heteralocha acutirostris*) An extinct bird, once favoured by Maori for its beautiful black plumage used to enhance weaving, and its prized white-tipped tail feathers – a favourite head decoration. As gifts, huia feathers were given to Queen Victoria's grandson, the Duke of York, who visited New Zealand in 1901, and he immediately placed them in his hat-band. Pictures of him wearing the huia feathers started a fashion in Britain. By then the bird was legally protected but that did not prevent skins being smuggled to Europe and sold. This, combined with the gradual destruction of forest areas, eventually brought doom to the huia: none has been seen since 1907. Contemporary Maori head-dress features a similar look, by using the tail feathers of turkeys.

I

I can do it in ...' A common response to a question about how far a destination is by car. The reply refers to the speaker's experience of the time it takes to do the drive. Such a claim may well be delivered with an element of machismo or boastfulness, so it is normally wise to regard the given time as exaggerated and add half an hour.

ice block Flavoured water, usually sweet, frozen onto a stick with which it is held. It is known elsewhere by various other names, such as popsicle, ice lolly.

iwi *Maori* All those to whom one is related by blood, tribe. In English the equivalent term would be kin, people to whom you are related by blood.

J

jack-up A clandestine arrangement that will procure an advantage for someone while retaining a fragile appearance of veracity. The imagery is from a car jack. The term has two meanings. (1) It can mean fixing-up, causing something effective to happen or a quite respectable arrangement to be made: *Barry jacked up a bridging loan until the house sale went through.* (2) It can be rather more shady, when something is wangled, contrived or engineered, usually to the advantage of whoever engineered it: *He jacked up the tickets so he could sit beside Jenny.*

jacky See **sitting up like jacky**

JAFA Acronym for a pejorative expression supposedly describing anyone living in Auckland as Just Another F . . . ing Aucklander.
(See **RONZ, Bombay Hills**)

Jaffa Trade name for a small spherical sweet with a chocolate core and a hard orange-flavoured coating. The name, registered to Sweetacres in 1951, comes from the colour of the oranges from the port of Jaffa in Israel.

jake, she'll be A substitute for okay, signifying that everything is going well, or will go well, and the result is expected to be pleasing. The reason for using jake is unknown – it may be related to the Scottish jake-easy, meaning amiable and agreeable, and have arrived in New Zealand with Scottish colonists.
(See **she'll be right**)

jandals Trade name for casual footwear made from rubber or plastic, in which the sole is held on by two side straps over the foot, which join at a short thong that passes between the big toe and the adjacent toe. They were the creation of a

New Zealand businessman called Anthony Yock, who had the idea in 1957 when he saw the Japanese *geta*, which has a sole (sometimes wooden) and a strap that passes around the big toe. He had a rubber version made and registered the trade name, which is an abbreviation of 'Japanese sandal'. Success was immediate and widespread. Imitators had to use a different name so throughout the world there are flip-flops, floppies and thongs; some Americans call them slippers; to the French they are known as Le Slap.

Janola Trade name for a widely used domestic bleach. The name is so familiar that it has come to mean any kind of bleach. It was named in honour of the originators' wives, Jan and Nola.

jelly Dessert made from flavoured and sweetened juices or liquids, set with gelatine. In the United States it is jello.

jetboat A fast-moving motor boat, propelled by water blasted from the stern, capable of travelling in shallow water and over rocky river beds. It was invented by New Zealand high country farmer Sir William Hamilton in 1954.

jigger (1) A lightweight conveyance especially constructed to carry one or two workmen along railway lines. It can be hand-propelled (by jigging a lever up and down, hence the name) or sometimes equipped with power drive. (2) A small glass to hold spirits.

joe, joey Informal term for a condom. Other words for the same item include johnny and raincoat. But joe should be treated with caution as it has different meanings in other countries. In Australia a joey is a baby kangaroo and the word is also used to mean a lie or a fake; a joe across the Tasman is also a ewe. In the United States a joe can mean just an ordinary man or a cup of coffee. In Britain a joe can sometimes mean a small silver coin, or a kind of canal boat.

joker An ordinary man, a bloke, a guy. The origin is a British slang word meaning both a jolly fellow (a joker) and an ordinary chap: Samuel Pepys used it that way in 1669. Since the 19th century the word has been used in Australia and New Zealand far more widely than anywhere else, and it is also sometimes applied to other living creatures, such as dogs.

Judas sheep A selected sheep kept in an abattoir, which has been taught to follow a certain path. Sheep brought in for slaughter are unsettled and cautious, but tend to follow a leader that appears to know what it is doing. Hence, as Judas historically betrayed Jesus, so the lead sheep leads the unknowing newcomers to the slaughter chain.

judder bar A low solid hump deliberately built across road surfaces that causes a juddering effect intended to discourage cars from driving dangerously fast. Americans call this a speed bump.

jug (1) A receptacle for fluids. It is widely used in New Zealand bars for dispensing draught beer, when the term refers to a jug filled with beer. (2) To jug. Attacking an opponent with a jug, either empty or full. Occasionally this piece of folklore is invoked in referring to a lively hostelry or sports team as The Flying Jug. (3) A cylindrical container of metal, ceramic or heavy plastic, electrified so as to raise cold tap water to boiling point – full name electric hot-water jug. (See **electric jug**)

just quietly Information given in confidential tones with a hidden proviso that the source should not be identified. It is sometimes also used jocularly, said with an air of pretend modesty when pronouncing something about oneself or another person which it is presumed might not be of general interest. *He said he was going to Taupo on business, but, just quietly, I think he has a girlfriend hidden there!*

K

kahawai *Maori* A popular fish, *Arripis trutta*, delicately coloured in blue-green, iridescent scales, offering both good eating, and good game in the catching. It is often both mispronounced and misspelled as kawai.

kai *Maori* Food, either in the general sense, or referring to a prepared and served meal. Kai moana is food from the sea.

kaka *Maori* A native New Zealand parrot, *Nestor meridionalis*. The bird is of considerable size, brownish in the North Island, greenish in the South Island, with some red feathers under the wings.

kakapo *Maori* A native New Zealand bird of the parrot family. *Strigops habroptilus* is somewhat bulky in build, ungainly and unable to fly – except to glide short distances downwards. The mossy green bird is rarely seen, being nocturnal and so nearly extinct that its exact numbers are constantly monitored. It has an unusual courtship ritual: to attract a partner it places itself in a bowl-shaped piece of territory, then utters a booming sound that can be heard at a distance.

Ka mate, ka mate *Maori* A haka, composed c.1820 by the great Ngati Toa chief Te Rauparaha. During a fierce battle with another chief, Te Rauparaha hid in a hirsute neighbour's kumara pit, concealed by the neighbour's wife. To be beneath a woman in this way was not a dignified situation for the great chief, who broke into a powerful oration before returning to the fight. Because it is used before sports matches, especially by the All Blacks, this is probably New Zealand's most famous haka. Unusually, it is in waltz rhythm.

Ka mate, ka mate!
Ka ora, ka ora!
Tenei te tangata puhuruhuru

Nana nei i tiki mei
I whakawhiti te ra!
Upane, upane!
Upane, ka upane
Whiti te ra!

Go away death,
Bring life,
There stands the hairy man
Who brought light to darkness
Take one upward step, one last upward step,
Then step forth – into the sun that shines!

kamokamo *Maori* The Maori name which has evolved to refer to the pumpkin-type plant *Cucurbita pepo* introduced into New Zealand during the 19th century. A tough-skinned type of gourd, it became a Maori delicacy, eaten when small with the skin a pale green colour, or as a tough-skinned reddish-orange gourd, with the cooked flesh scooped out. It quickly became established in New Zealand and was enthusiastically cultivated by Maori. Confusion over its name has resulted in such variations as cooma-cooma, kummy kum, kumukumu or kumikumi.

kapa haka *Maori* An inclusive term to describe the whole repertoire of performing arts within the Maori idiom – action songs, haka and waiata and poi songs.

kapai *Maori* A general term of approbation, affirming that all is well. In strict translation it means 'that good' (the Maori language has no verb to be). The word is frequently used in an English-language context.

karaka *Maori* A robust tree (*Corynocarpus laevigatus*) with large glossy green leaves and copious berries which ripen from green to clear orange, and contain a highly poisonous seed.

karakia *Maori* A similar concept to the English word prayer, but a karakia tends to be created afresh for a specific occasion, rather than having a ritualised regular structure.

karanga *Maori* A chanting call, usually performed by women, signifying the beginning of an event or gathering. Because such occasions generally take place outside, only women capable of producing this compelling sound are asked to give the karanga, which may offer information about the occasion, those attending and so on. The karanga is normally performed by one woman but on special occasions it becomes a two-person, or even a three-person, call.

Karitane *Maori* A name given to a system of hospitals and nurses focused on the needs of young mothers and children. They were founded by Sir Frederic Truby King, who also established, in 1907, the Society for the Promotion of the Health of Women and Children, soon rechristened the Plunket Society after the wife of the then governor. The name Karitane comes from the South Island district in which Sir Truby opened the first Karitane hospital, in his holiday home there; by the end of the 1920s there were six Karitane hospitals in New Zealand. The word Karitane became common usage to designate both the Karitane nurses trained throughout New Zealand in childcare, and the hospitals.

Less glamorously, the colour of excrement from young animals, particularly calves, is often described as Karitane yellow.

kaumatua *Maori* An elderly Maori man of dignity and good sense, whose opinions and advice are heeded by younger people. Only those deserving of the title are known as kaumatua.

kea *Maori* A native parrot, *Nestor notabilis*, found only in the South Island, generally in mountainous areas. Particularly bold, agile and noisy, kea have little fear of being close to humans and are markedly curious about their activities. It can be amusing to watch them tearing the tight foil off wrapped butter portions, or enjoying slides off a steep shiny roof, but their inquisitiveness can easily lead to destruction, such as stripping the rubber around a car windscreen in minutes. Hotels in kea territory have signs in the rooms advising that guests close all windows before going out of the room, or they may return to find their luggage demolished and any visible food eaten.

keg A barrel or cask made from either wood or aluminium, in which bulk fluid is kept until required, then withdrawn through a spigot or tap. Within New Zealand vernacular and according to the context, keg is frequently used to describe a considerable supply of beer, whether or not it comes from an actual keg.

kero *abbrev.* for kerosene.

kete *Maori* A bag, woven usually from strands of flax. The relationship with the English word kit is not clear, but it is believed that the New Zealand use of kit to mean a flexible carrying bag is a derivation from kete, rather than the other way round.

kia ora *Maori* A versatile Maori term of greeting and approbation. It is often thought to mean hello, but although it is used as a greeting it is more accurately translated as a 'hope for good health'. Kia ora and its wish for good health can also be applied to concepts or projects (e.g. a journey, a new job, a marriage) as well as to a person.

kick into touch To cause a deliberate break in proceedings that holds back a possibly disadvantageous action or decision and allows some time for reorganisation. The image is taken from rugby when a ball is, sometimes deliberately, kicked over the touch line, causing a short break in the game. *The resolution the chair wanted was just on the point of being passed but the accountant kicked the meeting into touch by asking that everyone be shown the state of the finances.*

kilikiti *Samoan* A lively Polynesian game based on cricket, as is the name, and played enthusiastically in many of the Pacific islands, including New Zealand. The basis of the game resembles traditional cricket, but teams may have 20 players, and the bat is something like a very large war club, three-sided, often well over a metre long and colourfully painted with tropical designs. Unlike traditional cricket, play is often interrupted by singing and dancing, and although competitiveness is not absent, a joyous time is had by all.

kina *Maori* Known in English as sea egg or sea urchin, *Evechinus chloroticus* is found in shallow sea waters. A flattened circle approximately 10 centimetres across and covered thickly with spines, kina are considered a great savoury delicacy. They are customarily steeped in fresh water for two days, then cracked open, and the tongue or roe inside is separated from the flesh, which is then mixed with cooked kumara and eaten. The roe is specially prized.

kindy Abbreviation of kindergarten.

King Country The western central part of the North Island, between Te Awamutu and Taupo. After the New Zealand Wars of the 1860s, when many Maori had their land confiscated, this area became their refuge and the centre of the Maori King Movement. (The first Maori king, Potatau, was crowned in 1858.) From then on the region, known to Maori as Rohe Potae, the rim of the hat, was informally referred to as the King's Territory, which later became King Country. The name became official in 1884. Until the end of the 19th century Pakeha were not welcome in the King Country.

King Dick A nickname for Richard Seddon, Premier of New Zealand from 1893 to 1906, originally coined by poet Thomas Bracken.

kiwi *Maori* A native bird, *Apteryx australis*, which is flightless, nocturnal, tailless, ground-feeding, short-sighted and with a very characteristic shape. The name is believed to be imitative of its cry. By 1887 the kiwi was being depicted in a university coat of arms, and by the start of the First World War the word, with a capital K, was widely used to describe New Zealand soldiers. It has grown since to become shorthand for sharemarket dollars, a furry fruit, boot polish, the national rugby league team and New Zealand citizens in general. During the 19th century, people then resident in New Zealand were known by such fanciful names as Fernlanders, Maorilanders and Moalanders, but kiwi is the identifying term that has stuck.

kiwiana Items that reflect New Zealand life and culture. The word was immortalised by researchers Richard Wolfe and Stephen Barnett in their book of that title, which revealed and paid tribute to surprising amounts of Kiwi ingenuity, advertising, customs, preferences and attitudes. Kiwiana, such as certain types of china and souvenirs, now commands high prices in antique and second-hand shops.

Kiwi battler A New Zealand-born person who has overcome adversity by a combination of optimism with enthusiasm for the work ethic.

kiwifruit A furry-skinned vine fruit with soft green, seeded flesh and a unique flavour. The fruit is Chinese in origin, from the Yangtze Valley, and has been grown in New Zealand since 1914. Under the name Chinese gooseberry, it was first exported to England in 1952. Later, when exports to the United States began, the name caused confusion so in 1959 the name kiwifruit was introduced by the Turner brothers, of the export firm Turners and Growers. The term won universal acceptance in a very short time; it is often shortened to kiwi. (See **Zespri**)

knock about, or **around** (1) Indulging in aimless activity. *At the weekend I should have finished my essay but I went out with friends and just knocked about instead.* (2) Being located somewhere nearby. *I've got a tin of paint stripper knocking around in the shed somewhere.*

knock off To finish, as in knocking off work. It can also mean to sell as in buying a new car and knocking off the old one. The term can also refer to a job that has been definitely completed, most famously by Sir Edmund Hillary after his ascent of Everest in 1953: *We knocked the bastard off.*

knock someone's block off To attack, and (figuratively) remove their head.
(See **block, do your block, use your block**)

knock up (1) To visit without prior arrangement (usually very early or very late – the door-knocking wakes them up), either friends you already know or strangers who happen to live close to where some emergency has happened. It can also refer to deliberately setting up a visit or a wake-up call in advance, such as asking a motel office to knock you up at 6 a.m. (2) To construct something in a hasty or temporary fashion, e.g. a shed (the same as knocked together). Most New Zealanders are aware that knock up has an entirely different meaning in other places, i.e. to make someone pregnant.

koha *Maori* A gift. It can be anything from a small, personal, individual present to a substantial donation of goods or money, which can, in some cases, be recognised legally as a form of tax-free transaction. Koha implies that something advantageous or pleasant is to be bestowed, without any payment being required. New Zealand museums that do not officially charge an entry fee sometimes ask for koha, a donation.

kohanga reo *Maori* A system established in 1982, where pre-school children are taught solely in the Maori language. The name has the literal meaning 'language nest'.

korero *Maori* Talk, in the sense of discussion, rather than just conversation (which is korerorero).

koro *Maori* A respectful term for an elderly man. It can also substitute for grandfather.

korowai *Maori* A hand-made traditional cloak. Woven from fine flax threads, or sometimes in pre-colonial times from stitched dog-skin, the cloaks can be strictly utilitarian, or art works of supreme beauty, decorated with feathers and tassels.

korry, py (pai) See **corry**

koru *Maori* A scrolled spiral shape depicting a stylised version of an uncurling young fern. The koru has been much used throughout Maori history, and borrowed by Pakeha: a form of the koru is the trademark of the national airline, Air New Zealand, and artist Gordon Walters employed it extensively in his work.

kotuku *Maori* A New Zealand native white heron (*Egretta alba modesta*), a bird of languid beauty which prefers a quiet life in the natural forest areas of the South Island's West Coast, most famously at Okarito. A Maori legend allows that good fortune may follow a (rare) sighting of a kotuku in flight.

kowhai *Maori* A native tree (*Sophora tetraptera*) with sparse and unspectacular foliage, but producing a vista of warm yellow blooms in spring. Hanging in groups, the tube-shaped blooms contain a sweet nectar at their base, strongly attractive to the native tui, which attend the trees in considerable numbers, singing their characteristic song.

kuia *Maori* An elderly Maori woman who is respected for her wisdom. The term is not automatically acquired simply by growing old, nor is it officially granted by any higher authority at a specific moment. To be a kuia is a state some women grow into gradually, as respect for them develops.

kumara *Maori* A sweet potato of South American origin, brought to New Zealand by whalers in the 1800s and now an established part of the food system. *The New Zealand Encyclopaedia* attributes the modern commercial kumara as being derived from that introduced from South America, rather than the different root vegetable brought earlier by Maori settlers. The most common variety is *Ipomoea batatas*, a member of the convolvulus family (kumara are not related to potatoes). The popular New Zealand type is large and plump, with a distinctive purple skin and pale gold flesh. Expatriate Kiwis have access to other sweet potatoes, such as Portuguese and contemporary South American, but declare they are not the same.

kumara short of a hangi (one)   A New Zealand version of the nonsense put-downs that include two sandwiches short of a picnic, two clowns short of a circus, a few bricks short of a load and a sausage short of a barbecue.

kumara vine   A New Zealand version of gossip being heard on the grapevine. The expression is used by Maori as a light-hearted description of the manner in which news travels through their own circles and communities, not always by conventional means. An equivalent occasionally heard is 'Maori tom-toms'.

kuri   *Maori* A dog. The word is sometimes mispronounced and misspelled, by non-Maori, as goorie.

kutu   *Maori* A nit, or louse – often the kind which gets into hair. It is frequently mispronounced and misspelled as cootie.

kybosh, kibosh   To organise a firm and unequivocal finish for a project, render a plan or an activity incapable of continuing. The word has been in English from the early 1900s, derived from the French *caboche* meaning to cut off the head – used literally by French hunters who had killed a deer, and figuratively by painters, when painting portraits that showed nothing below the shoulders. *Martin wanted to build another house on his section, but when they found that he planned to cut down several native trees, the council put the kybosh on his plan.*

L

Labour Day A public holiday on the last Monday in October. Although it is a day of leisure rather than labour, it was originally intended, when it began in 1899, to celebrate the acceptance of an eight-hour working day. The eight-hour day was not actually enshrined in law at that point, and only tradesmen and labourers were allowed the day off. Labour Day was observed on a Wednesday until 1910 when the day was changed.

ladies a plate A custom whereby women attending a social function would be asked to bring some food. The custom arose in New Zealand as a pragmatic demonstration that hospitality should be a shared responsibility. It was cheaper, too, than hiring a caterer and a normal practice in rural areas where there might not be any caterers. Sometimes providing a plate meant no entrance fee was required. The expression, which became widespread during the 1920s and remained in use throughout the 20th century, is famously confusing to overseas visitors or new immigrants.

lamb's fry Common name for the liver of lambs, sold for cooking. Although the meat is often prepared by frying, the name fry has tended to become a genteel substitute for the more pragmatic word liver, which some find distasteful. Note this should not be confused with lamb fries, which is an American term describing cooked testicles.
(See **mountain oysters**)

lamingtons Cubes of sponge, chocolate-coated and rolled in grated coconut. The recipe originated in Australia and its exact provenance is unclear, but the name is not: the cakes were named after Lord Lamington, Governor of New South Wales in 1896. Only 36 and keen on sports, he was popular with the Australians, who enjoyed his relaxed style. During his tenure, someone invented this delicacy. Julia Robinson, author of *Voices of Queensland*, reports that Lord Lamington referred to the cakes as 'bloody poofy' but nevertheless, because of his popularity, the confection was named after him and the lamington was born.

lash, have a   To make an enthusiastic attempt, to attempt an action energetically. Derived from the verb to lash, in its meaning of moving quickly with somewhat aggressive intent. *I'd never done a bunjy jump, and the height of the bridge terrified me, but I thought I'd have a lash at it anyway.*

laughing, to be away   Indicates a propitious beginning – that all preparations have been made, attitudes are positive and the project or activity will be successful. *We needed somewhere to rehearse and the community hall is available for eight Saturdays in a row, so we're away laughing.*

laughing gear   A mouth. The term was made popular, and maybe also invented by, author Barry Crump in the 1960s. *'Here,' said Bill, holding out a tray of freshly made scones, 'wrap your laughing gear around these.'*

lava lava   *Samoan* (in other Polynesian languages known as **sulu, pareu**) A Pacific wrap made of cloth or finely woven matting, worn around the waist and loins. The length of the lava lava from the waist downwards is sometimes governed by the gender of the wearer and the occasion at which it is being worn.

lay-by   Paying for a retail item by putting down a deposit and paying off the rest, usually in instalments. The term has been in use in New Zealand and Australia since the 1920s. In other countries, lay-by sometimes means a pausing space for motorists at the side of a busy road.

league   Rugby league. When some British rugby union clubs broke away from the Rugby Football Union in 1895, they called their new version of the game Northern Union. But in 1922 the name was altered to Rugby Football League, which gradually became just league. Even in rugby-mad New Zealand, league has gained in popularity over recent years, especially among the Maori and Pacific Island communities.

Lemon & Paeroa, L&P A carbonated, slightly acidulous and sweetened drink, made to the exact formula of the natural mineral waters found at the North Island town of Paeroa. Paeroa's fine mineral water was first analysed in 1904 and three years later, Menzies & Co. mixed lemon juice with it and created a national icon; as the advertising slogan says, the drink is 'world famous in New Zealand'. The original name was Paeroa and Lemon but it was reversed in 1914.

To avoid the cost of transporting the water to distant bottling plants, Menzies recreated an exact copy, using the chemical formula discovered during the 1904 analysis.

lift An enclosed platform or compartment in a vertical shaft which carries goods or people upwards and downwards. Americans prefer the term elevator; for them, lift means shoes for short people, or cosmetic surgery on the face.

like one thing An action or event of such extremity that nothing easily comes to mind with which to compare it. *The dog had seemed quite mild-tempered until it saw the rat, then went for it like one thing!*

lippy Boastful, arrogant, insolent and brash. The most common New Zealand use of the term mirrors the American use, established in the 1800s. Australia has developed a different version, which is also recognised on this side of the Tasman: there lippy is shorthand for lipstick. There is a subtle distinction between being insolent – lippy – and simply being too talkative. Generally, when the meaning is 'talking too much', New Zealanders use the word 'mouthy'.

Lockwood, a A building, usually a house, made from pre-cut sections which are assembled on site. Lockwood is a trade name for the enterprise Lockwood International Ltd, which was established in Rotorua in 1951.

Log of wood A fanciful nickname for the inter-provincial rugby trophy, the Ranfurly Shield.

lolly *abbrev.* Lollipop. Spelt as lolly or lollie, this has been a widespread New Zealand term for almost any kind of confectionery since about 1860. Sometimes a slightly more pragmatic alternative is used – chews. Also used, in the past, was lolly water (curiously, also known as soft drink). The informal expression 'toss your lollies' means to vomit. In Britain lollies are sweets.

lolly scramble Casting a wide throw of lollies for children to race after and retrieve – a popular feature at school fairs, sports events etc. The image has become a metaphor for any advantageous situation in business or government, for which there is considerable competition among those who foresee gains in wealth, power or status.

long drop An outdoor lavatory with a seat built over a very deep hole. A long drop is formally known as a deep trench latrine or earth closet. In the era before flush toilets were available in New Zealand, or in areas where their use was impractical, two kinds of outdoor toilet evolved. One involved a seat fitted to a generously sized metal can, which was emptied at intervals, maybe even by the night soil man with his cart. The alternative was a long drop.

loo A substitute word for lavatory, toilet. The word's origin has never been absolutely clarified – perhaps the French *lieux d'aisance*, water closet – but it is accepted as the most graceful of a long list of substitutes in New Zealand for lavatory: restroom, bog, crapper, grot, dunny, head, shithouse, WC, khazi, la-la, outhouse, long drop and, very rarely, the privy, the can or the john.

loose metal The surface of a road, usually rural, on which broken stones have been spread, without being bound together in asphalt or any other medium.
(See **metal**)

lorry A large truck. The word has been traced to a Yorkshire and Lancashire dialect word *lurry* meaning to pull and applied to a flat dray. It is possibly influenced by another dialect word *rolley*, for a coal-mining truck – hence something that moves along by rolling.

luck out (1) To be beset with bad fortune and a succession of mishaps. (2) To be blessed with unexpected advantage. Australia and New Zealand tend to follow (1) while the United States embraces (2). *Ernie used his whole bonus cheque on the bet but he lucked out and the horse came in seventh.*

luncheon sausage Finely ground meat, pre-cooked, flavoured and packed into a very large sausage shape, from which slices are cut to be eaten cold. Once known as German sausage.

lurk An ingenious and often novel scheme, unconventional and possibly fraudulent, which results in profit for the perpetrator. The image seems to be related to the word's usual meaning of prowling quietly applied to a business practice that hovers discreetly on the outer edges of mainstream business activity. *He had a great lurk going: he bred dozens of white mice in his garden shed, then sold them to medical laboratories.*

M

mad (1) Impolite reference to anyone suffering from mental illness. (2) Angry – followed by nonsense qualifiers such as mad as a meat-axe or mad as a snake.

mad as a gumdigger's dog Silly, showing little sign of normal commonsense. Images concerning gum-digging arose during the period when kauri gum was dug for, particularly in the north of the North Island, and used for a variety of purposes. Gumdigger's soap was a kind of flower that lathered when scrunched and gumdigger's spud was the edible bulb of a New Zealand orchid. The dogs living in the tough gumfields environment would not have been elegant creatures, and dogs are renowned for their loyalty and keenness to forage, so a combination of all these factors is the probable origin of skinny as a gumdigger's dog, useless as a gumdigger's dog and mad (meaning silly) as a gumdigger's dog.

maggoty Tetchy, short-tempered, easily irritated. The term is inappropriate in that real maggots show little sign of temper and even if they did, couldn't wreak much damage. But the inescapable aura of unpleasantness which hovers over the maggot does duty for the metaphor.

maimai Little makeshift huts or primitive temporary covering, constructed near water, partly for shelter and partly for concealment. The name is not Maori, but from the Western Australian Nyungar Aboriginal language and was originally miamia. The word has been used in New Zealand since the 1860s when European settlers saw Maori shelters made from sticks covered with hastily woven raupo and fern. Eventually the vowels reversed into maimai. During the gold rush, prospectors reluctant to leave a claim would build a maimai for themselves; New Zealand soldiers constructed maimais at Gallipoli. Since the 1930s, maimais have been most associated with duck-shooters, who use the word to describe their little huts, built near water.

main, main course, mains The principal dish of a meal, as opposed to the smaller snack – the starter, appetiser or entrée – that begins a three-course meal. The plural occurs when a restaurant lists all its principal dishes.
(See **entrée**)

Mainland, the A common term for the South Island of New Zealand. Since it is the biggest of the islands which form New Zealand, theoretically it is the main island and all the others are subsidiary. In the 19th century the South Island was the centre of prosperity, though not of politics, so the term Mainland may have been understood for decades before it went into popular parlance. When touring New Zealand in 1947, Field Marshal Lord Montgomery was cheered when he referred to the South Island as the Mainland. Legend says that this was the first public utterance of the expression. Canterbury-born Prime Minister Holland used it often between 1949 and 1957 and by 1960 it was widely recognised.

mako *Maori* A variety of shark, *Isurus oxyrinchus*, with considerable reputation as a big game fish. One captured example, in the Auckland Museum, is nearly 4 metres long and weighed more than 350 kilograms. The species is found around both New Zealand and Australia, where it is known as a blue pointer, or sometimes as snapper shark. The teeth were a prized traditional ornament for Maori.

mall A collection of shops in a planned, self-contained group. Mall is derived from pall mall, an Italian mallet and ball game called *palla a maglio* which became popular in London and gave its name to the places where it was played: Pall Mall and the Mall. The word mall became associated with space and pleasant walking. In 1967 the word mall was used in the United States to refer to a shopping centre and now it is commonplace.

In New Zealand mall is pronounced to rhyme with brawl.

mana *Maori* A combination of dignity, prestige, influence and possibly power. No single English word equates exactly with the Maori term. Mana, which may be possessed by an individual person or a group, is not actually bestowed but accumulates subtly over time. Although the prestige and rank of a person of mana is clearly recognised by others, it is not usually claimed for oneself.

manuhiri *Maori* Visitor, especially in formal context, such as when visiting a marae. The people who belong to that marae are said to have a place for their feet; visitors are customarily accorded a formal welcome or powhiri, after which their feet, and hence their persons, are accepted among the hosts.

manuka *Maori* A small tree (*Leptospermum scoparium*) widespread in most of New Zealand. Often spindly and somewhat cramped-looking in growth, and without particularly notable leaves, the tree is not attractive in itself, but yields excellent firewood, bark with medicinal qualities and tiny but pretty summer flowers from which comes the very desirable manuka honey, which is both delicious and very good for one's health.

Maori *Maori* The indigenous Polynesian people of New Zealand. There is some doubt as to what the word originally meant, though 'normal people' seems the most probable, as Maori lived in comparative isolation and did not require a word to describe themselves. To get as close as possible to the correct pronunciation, think 'mowrie'.

Maori bread A type of bread, usually made with a form of yeast derived from potatoes. It is rich in texture and full of flavour but must be eaten fresh. There are several varieties, the most popular being rewena.

Maori land Freehold land held in ownership by Maori groups or families with tenancy in common, under legal customary right. The ownership can be multiple, since by ancient Maori custom land is frequently jointly owned by a group of people, possibly an entire tribe.

Maori Queen The female head of the Maori King Movement. This began in 1 June 1858 with the coronation of the first Maori King, Potatau. The role normally passes down through blood descendants: the current incumbent, since 1966, is the daughter of the late King Koroki, and assumed the name Te Ata Irangikaahu on her enthronement. Her title among her people is Te Arikinui (Great Chief) and in 1970 Queen Elizabeth raised her to the damehood.
(See **Arikinui**)

Maoritanga *Maori* The unique practices, rituals and knowledge thereof, language, culture and beliefs that collectively make up the philosophies and practicalities of Maori life.

Maori time A Maori attitude to time, which is more relaxed than that of Europeans. The term is frequently regarded as at least slightly offensive. In 1948, the late Prof. Ernest Beaglehole defined the Pakeha concept of time as 'something solid, fixed and definite, to which other activities must be geared', contrasting it with the Maori concept, which is of 'a plastic medium that flows around and adapts itself to the activities of the day'.

marae *Maori* Strictly the open piece of land in front of the wharenui (meeting house), though modern general usage tends to describe the entire complex of buildings and land as a marae. Although it is used for meetings and social occasions, a marae has a much greater ceremonial significance: as a centre of tribal (family) life, it is a place for welcoming visitors, for holding tangi or funerals, for hosting vigorous formally structured meetings. In European terms a marae sits somewhere between, and combines the roles of a parliament, a church and a village green.

marching girls Young New Zealand women executing display marching while wearing quasi-military costume. A New Zealand invention, originally called girls' drill, it was first observed during a 1901 royal visit. Within two decades the activity had become an organised sport and it continued to flourish. The first competitions were held in 1933 and by 1944 a formal Marching Association set codes of rules and costume. By 1980 there were over 350 marching girl teams. Now called drill teams, marching girls have become much less popular.

maritime park The term no longer has official standing, but is widely used without necessarily acknowledging the differences between the two current official terms: (1) marine reserve: a ministerially sanctioned area of territorial water from which nothing can be taken and which is disturbed as little as possible so that the eco-system can be maintained in its natural state, and (2) maritime park: an area of territorial water that may be administered by the Ministry of Fisheries and harbour boards, or by its own individual legislation; its protective measures are not as stringent as those for a marine reserve.

matai *Maori* A tree sometimes known as black pine (*Podocarpus spicatus*), which produces a quality timber notable for its durability and often found in flooring.

Matariki *Maori* The mid-year appearance of the seven-star constellation of Pleiades, known in Maori as Te Paki o Matariki, which signalled to Maori that the yearly cycle of winter followed by summer was under way. Traditionally the stars of Matariki signalled the time for laying down foods for the cold months, such as dried fish and stored kumara, and also preparing for the way ahead by planting kumara.

Some festivities still occur to mark the occasion, which is often referred to as the Maori New Year, in much the same spirit as European customs that marked the turn of winter and celebrated the recognition that warmer months would eventually come.

mates' rates An informal arrangement by which goods or services are obtained at a reduced price, based on the relationship between those involved. The links may include friendship, family relationship, former membership of the same school, army or sports organisations. *Adding our extra bedroom would have cost a packet, but the wife has a cousin who's a builder so we got mates' rates.*

mauri *Maori* The guiding principle of human life, the talisman within each person that is their personality and life force. The word is often heard in the beginning of a Maori speech: Tihei mauri ora – Behold, there is life. The term arises from the legendary breath that was put into the first created woman. Mauri should not be confused with Maori – they are not pronounced in the same way.

meat safe A box-like cupboard for meat and other perishables, either mounted separately outside, or actually built into the coolest part of the house, with one side fitted with fine wire netting to allow air flow but keep flies out. The netting is sometimes fitted with wooden angle-slatting to prevent sunlight getting in. In post-refrigeration years the word is seldom heard, but in former times every kitchen revolved around the safe, and some isolated bush huts still use one.

mere *Maori* A short flat club with a characteristic ovoid shape and sharpened edge, made from bone, greenstone or stone. Unlike a thick club which is used to bludgeon, the deadliness of the mere lies in its edge, used in battle for side-striking or forward-lunging, at vulnerable body parts.
(See **patu**)

messages, doing the New Zealand shorthand for the quick shopping necessary for the household's daily needs. Other nationalities do the errands or the marketing.

metal Broken stone used for road-making. Many New Zealand country roads are surfaced with rocks and stones that have been crushed and broken, but not sealed. They are customarily referred to as metal roads – a term that can puzzle overseas visitors.

mihi *Maori* A greeting. It may follow a ritual, depending on the circumstances, but is less elaborate and formal than a ceremonial powhiri.

MMP *abbrev.* Mixed Member Proportional, the electoral system in New Zealand since 1996, which allows each eligible voter two votes – one for the favoured candidate in that electorate area, the other for the political party the elector chooses to support.

moa *Maori* A large, flightless bird (*Dinornithiformes*), now extinct, one species of which grew up to 3 metres tall. They are thought to have lived in New Zealand for millions of years. When Maori people arrived in New Zealand, they found the bird's flesh, bones, skin, feathers and eggs very useful – the flesh for meat, the skins and feathers for garments and decoration, the bones for implements and the huge eggshells for water bottles. The moa was hunted out of existence and by approximately AD 1500 was seen no more.

mocker An informal expression meaning clothes. The term's origin is mysterious.

moko *Maori* (1) Traditional body tattooing, usually facial. The patterns are incised into the flesh and permanently coloured. Among pre-20th-century Maori, and today, facial and body tattooing followed strictly observed rituals and designs. The intricate designs can convey a person's ancestry, rank, family and legendary connections. Moko on men can cover a large area of the face, women's moko is generally confined to the chin and lips. (2) The word is also heard as an abbreviation of mokopuna (see below). (3) Less commonly, moko can also mean lizard.

mokopuna *Maori* A grandchild. Besides blood relatives, the word is also sometimes used to indicate a wider group of young children, not necessarily one's own. The word is often abbreviated to moko.

Mondayised Moving a statutory holiday such as Labour Day so that it always falls on a Monday, regardless of whether it falls on the exact date being commemorated.

money for jam Easy profit requiring little risk or effort. The term is similar to 'money for old rope', which developed from the practice of collecting and selling bits of rope from sailing ships for caulking. The only known reason for the jam version is the large amounts of jam made by British housewives during the First World War and sent to the troops as a morale booster. Since the war did not affect fruit growing, this jam-making somehow later gained a connotation of being a product achieved without great outlay. Although often heard in New Zealand, the jam version is not widely used elsewhere.

Mooloo A mock-up figure of a cow which initially represented Waikato's dairy industry, then was taken up in 1952 by supporters of local sports teams, and has gradually has become a by-word for anything referring to the Waikato.

morepork A nocturnal native owl, whose proper name is *Ninox novaseelandiae*. Its English name is derived from the sound it seems to make during its night-time calling. Maori call the bird ruru, a name that echoes the sound the bird's call makes to Maori ears. The birds quite frequently venture into urban areas, but because they fly very quietly, and only at night, they are seldom seen.

Moriori *Maori* The name given to a Polynesian group which some scholars believe may have arrived in New Zealand prior to the Maori arrival, but who were gradually overwhelmed by stronger factions. The word has had many spellings and pronunciations, and may be a regional or corrupted version of *Maori*.

morning tea A short break from work, at which tea (or coffee) is drunk, often with a biscuit. Morning tea can also be a more defined social occasion to which people (often women) are invited and at which a wide variety of food, such as biscuits, cakes, scones and muffins, is served.

mountain oysters Testicles from young male calves, cleaned, peeled and fried. In Spanish they are called eggs of the bull. Another name variant is prairie oysters, which can also describe an egg yolk swallowed whole with lemon juice and pepper.
(See **lamb's fry**)

mousetrap A savoury snack or light meal, made from bread topped with chutney and grated cheese, then toasted in an oven. Mousetrap is also commonly used in recipes to describe ordinary cheese.

mozzie *abbrev.* of mosquito.

muck around (1) Doing nothing in particular in a leisurely sense. (2) Occupying your time but not achieving anything when you should be. Someone can end up mucking around in the first sense because someone is mucking around in the second sense. *I couldn't get anyone to serve me. The staff all seemed to be mucking around, not paying any attention to the customers.*
(See **stuff around**)

mudguard The curved metal cover over a car wheel that prevents water and mud from being splashed upwards as the vehicle travels along. Elsewhere they are sometimes called wings.

mum *abbrev.* of mother, but in New Zealand the term is also frequently used by men referring to their wives. This is judged to reflect an early social trend, especially in rural New Zealand, where a man lived with his parents until he found a wife and transferred the nomenclature for one woman to the other.

muster The collecting together of livestock, when counting is due, or branding. Sometimes used informally to describe a meeting of people.

muttonbirds Various seabirds, mainly the sooty shearwater and the grey-faced petrel, which are eaten, especially by Maori (who call them titi). The flesh when cooking has a mutton-like smell. Cooked in their own fat, which also preserves them, the birds have long been considered a delicacy by Maori and were traded throughout the country. The birds also gave their name to a New Zealand music group, The Muttonbirds.

mutton flap A thick slice taken from the belly of a slaughtered sheep (similarly sometimes lamb flap) which is inexpensive but very high in fat and not encouraged by nutritionists.

N

Naki, the *abbrev.* of the name of the province, Taranaki. Fortunately the quirky short form cannot cause offence, since tara in Maori means peak, but naki has never been clearly defined.

nana, nan, nanny A way of referring to a grandmother. The term nanny in the British sense of a professional child-minder used to be rare in New Zealand, but is now becoming more common.

nappy, nap *abbrev.* for babies' napkin. American babies are kept clean by being folded into diapers (derived from a medieval Greek word meaning 'pure white') but New Zealand has stuck with napkin, and typically abbreviated it to nappy or simply nap. Suburbs containing many young households with babies are sometimes jokingly referred to as *Nappy Valley*.

The word 'napkin' is occasionally used to refer to the folded linen variety found at elegant dinner parties.

never-never (1) A euphemism for time payment or hire purchase, when a desired article is paid for in instalments but is already being used. (2) A shortened form of J. M. Barrie's Never-Never Land, the home of Peter Pan – thus as an expression referring to an inaccessible district far away from urban activity. *She's put a dishwasher and a fancy microwave into her kitchen, but she's paying them off on the never-never.*

next (1) immediately adjacent. (2) On New Zealand television and radio, next means after the commercials.

ngati *Maori* One of its meanings is 'the descendants of' so the word can be heard prefacing the name of a tribe: Ngati Porou, for example, are the descendants of Porourangi. The word is also used to mean 'the' before a collective noun.

nibbles Small food items on trays or in bowls, served, usually with drinks, at a social function where there is no actual meal. Nibbles are also often called finger food, denoting that a knife and fork (and often a plate) are not needed.

nick, in the To be nude. The term is believed to be a variant on naked or nix, meaning nothing – by extension, wearing nothing. There seems to be no connection with in the nick, meaning prison.

niggly Impatient, critical, short-tempered, fractious, fussy. Niggly comes from a Norwegian word, *nigla*. In its sense of pernickety or nagging, niggly is commonly used in New Zealand.

night's still a pup, the A popular way of saying that there are several hours to go before daybreak so the festivities can continue.

nikau A type of palm tree (*Rhopalostylis sapida*) native to New Zealand. Its stem or trunk often grows with a swollen area at the leaf junction and from this stem top can be extracted a juicy flesh for eating.

ning-nong A foolish person. The term is derived from 'nincompoop' with some influence from the military slang term 'nig-nog', meaning a fool. It is sometimes abbreviated to just nong.

No Circulars A sign on letter-boxes warning that unsolicited advertising materials are not welcome, although the defiant distribution of such material is difficult to prevent. The practice attracts legal argument balancing the right of advertisers to distribute their material, against that of householders who wish to receive only mail that is actually addressed to them.

no-hoper A person who is ineffectual and incompetent. The term has been shared between New Zealand and Australia since the 1940s.

no kidding (1) Interrogative: Are you telling the truth? (2) Affirmative: I am telling the truth. The difference between the two is easily judged by the context and vocal tone. Kidding, meaning joking and teasing, and originally used in the United States, is possibly an imitative term arising from the tendency of young goats (kids) to frisk about with an impertinent look on their faces.

North Cape to Bluff A picturesque way of saying the entire country of New Zealand, from its northernmost to its southernmost tip (though it leaves out Stewart Island). Its equivalent in Britain would be from John O'Groats to Land's End.

nosey, a (1) A comprehensive but clandestine look around, and (2) the act of doing so: having a nosey. *She said she wanted to use the loo but I think she just wanted a nosey at the rest of the house.*

nosey parker A person who either (1) enquires too deeply into matters that do not concern them but might make for interesting tattle elsewhere, or (2) makes an effort to examine places and people when there is little valid reason to do so except blatant curiosity.

notornis See **takahe**

no worries This means exactly what it says: it is a shorthand way of indicating confidence and competence that something can be accomplished with ease. Although originally an Australian expression, it has become popular on this side of the Tasman. *When I told the mechanic I needed the car back by evening, he said, 'No worries'.*

nugget (1) A small lump of something in its natural state (e.g.

gold, coal, gum). As an adjective, nuggety, it is used to describe a person or animal who is stocky and not tall. (2) The name Nugget was patented for use in New Zealand in 1903, as a leather preservative; it had originated in Britain. The name may have arisen because Nugget was originally black and sold in lumps. Within a decade nugget had become a general New Zealand term for shoe polish, and the verb to nugget – to polish – your shoes developed.

nui *Maori* Big. When it is required to describe something as very big, the word simply doubles: nuinui.

Number eight (No. 8) wire A by-word for making an ingenious repair with materials close to hand. For many years the favoured wire for New Zealand fencing was No. 8, which was widely available and known for its strength. Because it was often used for fixing other things, especially mechanical, the phrase No. 8 fencing wire became a synonym for such repairs and remains so, even though the original wire is far less common these days.

nuts See **going nuts**

O

Oamaru stone A limestone quarried from hills in the eastern region of North Otago in the South Island. Over a period of thousands, perhaps millions, of years, calciferous marine shells on the sea floor hardened and, when eventually lifted above sea level, were revealed to have become a beautiful creamy-white coloured stone, with a suitable texture for building. The port town of Oamaru is rich in splendid historic buildings made from the stone.

Oceania The geographic area around New Zealand and including it. Commonly used, especially in Europe, the term is almost never used in New Zealand except in the name for a sporting event, e.g. Oceania Games. Oceania loosely means the islands of the central and south Pacific including Melanesia, Polynesia and Micronesia, sometimes also including Australia and the Malay Archipelago. New Zealanders prefer to say the Pacific or the South Pacific.

ocker Informal term for an Australian. The word is based on a nickname for anyone called Oscar, and appeared as such in a 1920s Australian magazine cartoon series called *Ginger Meggs*, in which one character was called Ocker Stevens. This led to a practice of calling anyone Ocker whose surname was Stevens. The word gained more prominence in 1965, when actor Ron Frazer created a character called Ocker on a television satire programme *The Mavis Bramston Show*. Initially the term described an Australian male who was loud-mouthed and devoid of grace, but time has softened the definition.
(See **Oz**)

odd (1) Unusual, peculiar: *He was an odd person, who behaved a little bit strangely.* (2) Random, occasional: *After the knitting was finished, some odd bits of wool were left over.* New Zealand has embraced the second meaning. Weather reports predict odd showers, which means they will be unpredictable and occasional, not peculiar. A person who experiences the odd spot of bother is one who lands in trouble from time to time.

OE *abbrev.* Overseas Experience. Because they live in such a geographically isolated country, many New Zealanders travel extensively, often in their 20s by backpacking or hitchhiking, to experience how the rest of the world lives. Some never come back; others do so happily. The popular abbreviation OE was coined by the father of Massey University lecturer, John Muirhead, who used it in the 1960s. Writer and cartoonist Tom Scott heard it when he was a student at Massey and later used the term freely in his *Listener* column, and it rapidly became a part of the language. If someone is away for a year or more, they are often said to be on or doing the big OE.

offshore Foreign, overseas. Strictly, offshore means out in the sea, not too far from the shore, as for oil rigs, but the word has also evolved the extra use.

oil The truth, especially when expressed as the dinkum – also good, real and right – oil, which is the absolute truth. The term is believed to have arisen in prospecting fields where the lucky person who found oil discovered there was truth in his hopes and dreams.

oily rag, to live on the smell of an A frugal existence, bordering on poverty, with insufficient income for anything but the most basic of food and conditions. The saying existed in Ireland before 1910 and later, when cars became common, motorists rapidly took up the expression to demonstrate how economic their cars were with petrol. Gradually the term broadened to include any lifestyle or set of habits that were financially straitened.

on the knocker Punctual, prompt, accurate. The expression, believed to be Australasian in origin, compares these qualities to the brisk rat-tat-tatting on a door.

on the pig's back To be in a fortunate or happy position, to have found success.

op shop *abbrev.* of opportunity shop, the name customarily used by charity organisations for a shop, staffed by volunteers, which sells donated, usually used, clothes and goods.

outage Breakdown, or lacking something vital. The term arose in the United States, at first when items from a big shipment mysteriously went missing. The word became fashionable and was used to describe difficulties with telephones, an electric power cut or a computer malfunction. The word gradually found favour in New Zealand, especially in the 21st century. In some inexplicable way, the term seems to remove blame: there has not been a breakdown and no one has made a mistake.
(See **power cut**)

out of one's tree Drunk, or in some other way out of control.

out of whack Unbalanced, uneven, not a neat fit. In practical terms the expression can describe asymmetrical carpentry or engineering but is also often used figuratively to describe a project, or set of ideas, that does not sit comfortably in its context. *Everything she suggested to the committee was out of whack with the majority feeling.*

overseas funds Monies held in a country outside New Zealand (e.g. through inheritance, shares, earnings from working there) and retained to be accessed from New Zealand, either to purchase and import goods unavailable at home, or to utilise when travelling in that country.

overstayer A person who has remained in the country past the date their visa allows, and thus risks being declared an illegal immigrant.

(See **dawn raid**)

Oz Informal reference to Australia. New Zealanders have long referred to Australia and Australians as Aussie/Aussies and over time this became abbreviated to Oz, like the home of the famous wizard. Oz is used only for the country; the inhabitants are still called Aussies.

(See **ocker**)

P

pa, pah *Maori* Traditionally a pa was a communal settlement, a Maori village. Usually placed in a strategic part of the countryside, a pa was often fortified against attack. By the mid-20th century, Maori families were tending to live in cities, and the word went out of common use. Maori families all retained strong family and spiritual connections to the sacred piece of open land, the marae, around which all village and tribal matters were administered, and the large meeting house attached to it, the wharenui.
(See **marae, wharenui**)

pack See **gone to the pack**

pack a sad Initially dating from about 1980, the expression described anyone who was upset, seeking help and sympathy or remaining silent in the face of depressing news, but it came to be used for non-human malfunction or a condition causing displeasure. *Cancelling the cricket match on Saturday was a real bummer, but the pitch had packed a sad because of the rain and there was no way we could play.*

paddock An area of open land that is fenced, usually for farming purposes. In Britain, the word is usually associated with horse-racing, while farms are made up of meadows or fields. New Zealanders also sometimes refer to a rugby field as the paddock.

pakaru *Maori* Broken, ruined, not able to function. The word was quickly taken up by Europeans and first appeared in print in 1820. During the 19th century the word was spelt several different ways: pakadu, pukeru, buckeroo and, most commonly, puckaroo. The word is also used as a verb – to be pakaru'd. Maori pronounce pakaru with the emphasis on the first syllable whereas European New Zealanders tend to place the stress on the last syllable.

Pakeha *Maori* New Zealand residents who are not Polynesian. The word was originally used by Maori to distinguish Europeans from themselves. Its exact origin and meaning have been discussed and examined for decades, and while many explanations have been put forward, none is universally accepted. Rightly or wrongly, the word is believed by some to have derogatory connotations – and it is probably true to say that the word is used less often by non-Maori New Zealanders than it once was.

palagi *Samoan* A European or non-Samoan. The literal translation is 'sky people': when Samoans first saw non-Polynesians, they thought they must have come down from the sky. The pronunciation, *pa-langi*, requires acknowledgement of the hidden consonants that occur in some Polynesian and Melanesian languages.

panel beater Someone who restores damaged parts of a car exterior to their proper shape. The term is unfamiliar and amusing to some visitors, but New Zealanders find the American equivalent, body shop, equally funny.

paper lolly Small individual pieces of confectionery, each enclosed in folded paper (usually waxed paper or cellophane). Paper lollies are known elsewhere as wrapped sweets.
(See **lolly**)

Parnell shout Each person in a group paying for their own drinks. The term arose in the Auckland suburb of Parnell about the time of the First World War when impoverished local literary types could rarely afford to buy drinks for someone else.
(See **shout**)

part up with Giving up (often reluctantly) goods or money either owed or required by obligation for some purpose.

party pooper The person whose unwillingness to participate in or continue some festive activity causes a blight to fall on the proceedings, disappointing the other participants.

passing lane A portion of a road or motorway designated for passing only.

patu *Maori* A hand-held weapon, wielded like a club and lethal when used in battle. Now seen only in museums, or during ceremonials and rituals.

paua *Maori* A New Zealand shellfish, *Haliotis iris*. It is valuable both for the lovely iridescent colouring of its generously-sized shell and for its black flesh, which is beaten vigorously and cooked to make an interesting seafood. Although different in colouring, the paua is closely related to the North American abalone, which is more bland in appearance. Polished paua shell glows in marine colours and is widely used as decoration in traditional Maori carvings (particularly as the 'eyes' in humanoid figures) and also as a contemporary design feature in fashion, fabrics, tiles, interior design, sculpture and jewellery. Gathering paua from the sea is subject to rigid conservation-conscious rules regarding size, method and amount.

pavlova A meringue dessert, usually topped with whipped cream and some sliced fruit. The word meringue comes from the German district of Mehr-in-Yghen where, several centuries ago, a dish was made using egg whites baked with sugar. The New Zealand version of the dessert takes its name from the famous Russian ballerina Anna Pavlova, who danced in New Zealand in 1926. The first recipe with that name appeared in New Zealand in 1929.

peggy square A small square of knitted or crocheted wool, of which a great number are stitched together to assemble a large rug. The practice was named after four-year-old Peggy Huse of Wellington, who in 1930 used left-over wool to knit several squares into a cover for a doll's cradle. A local broadcaster saw her doing so and suggested that this might be a way of providing blankets for children who needed them during the Depression. Details of how to make the squares were broadcast over the radio and the idea caught on. It has been a charitable fund-raiser ever since.

perf A payment made by the police to a member of the force obliged to retire early for medical reasons (sometimes cynically perceived as not being genuine). The action of doing so is to perf out. The word comes from the initials of the Police Employment Rehabilitation Fund.

perk, perkbuster *abbrev.* of perquisite, an incidental advantage or benefit, in finance or in kind (such as the use of a car), which is discreetly attached to a more transparent salary or honorarium. A perkbuster exposes such arrangements to public view, especially when they involve questionable use of taxpayers' money.

perv, to perv, perve *abbrev.* of pervert. (1) A person whose moral and sexual standards differ from what is regarded as the norm, and attracts criticism for that reason. (2) A salacious viewing by outsiders of activities normally acknowledged as private. (3) The act of watching something with prurient interest, as in a peeping Tom.

picnic A difficult situation, a problematical set of events resulting in a series of difficulties. The word used in this sense is probably of ironic origin – its meaning a deliberate contrast to the happy occasion of a real picnic. Elsewhere the term 'pretty kettle of fish' fulfils the same purpose. *Apparently before we arrived, the kids had locked the garage door, the dog had disappeared, the street had no water and the stove elements had burnt out, so we stumbled into a real picnic!*

pie In New Zealand a pie is for individual eating, a one-stop meal. Elsewhere the word more commonly refers to a much larger offering, from which slices are cut for individual people to eat. New Zealanders buy a pie lunch or as a snack. The British version, the individual pork pie, has a surprisingly low profile in New Zealand.

pie cart A long low-slung caravan which parks in the same position in an urban street each night and serves takeaway food such as hot pies with mashed potatoes and peas, and hamburgers.

piece of piss, a piss in, piss in the hand See **piss**

pie, pea and pud An all-in-one casual meal consisting of a meat pie combined with mashed potatoes and cooked peas (pud here is an abbreviation of spuds). An Australia pie floater is marginally different, being a bowl of thick split-pea soup in the middle of which floats a whole pie, topped with tomato sauce.

Pig Islander An informal name for a New Zealander, which can be considered to be in doubtful taste. It is believed to originate in Captain Cook's 1769 introduction of domestic pigs to New Zealand. Many of them escaped, so that an impression somehow grew of a country rich in wild pigs – the Pig Islands. In 1966 the well-known poet James K. Baxter published a collection of poetry entitled *Pig Island Letters*.

pikelet A small, round, pancake-like snack, made from batter which includes leavening, dropped directly onto a hot cooking surface, then turned and cooked on the other side. It is best eaten within ten minutes of being cooked, with butter, jam and cream. Pikelets are known in other parts of the world as drop scones or girdle scones.

piker One who shirks, is timid and ventures little. The word has a 1930 American origin – a person to be scorned because they duck responsibility, or who leave parties early. You can therefore pike or pike out.

pipi *Maori* A small shellfish, *Paphies australis*, prolific on New Zealand beaches. Often dismissed as unworthy in gastronomic value, pipi are nevertheless accounted a novelty treat after they have been simmered or steamed.

piss A number of expressions are based on the earthy assumption that urinating is normally very easy to do. Hence piece of piss (a variation on the expression piece of cake), a piss in and piss in the hand refer to an easily achieved victory, a task performed with success and without difficulty. Piss over carries the same meaning – but with the added connotation that in achieving the easy success, one has caused some grief to the other competitor(s). Piss in the pocket describes sycophancy, unnecessary attention to someone in authority, in order to gain advancement.

pissed, pissed off The two terms have quite different applications in New Zealand. Pissed means drunk, but pissed off means disgruntled and angry. Americans customarily use the shorter version 'pissed' on its own to mean angry, which can cause confusion in New Zealand.

piupiu *Maori* A skirt-like garment, consisting of a fringe made from many strands of dried flax suspended from a waistband, worn as native costume by men (short strands) and women (long strands). The flax leaves are harvested while still green, then notches are cut into the individual strands, which are scraped to expose the fibres: the notches are planned to create symmetrical decorative designs. The flax strands are then boiled in black mud and, when dried, become tubular in shape. The scraped portions will have turned black. The designs now revealed have an affiliation to the art-heritage of the wearer's tribe.

piwakawaka *Maori* See **fantail**

play lunch A snack eaten during a mid-morning school break, and usually provided from home but also available in some schools' tuck shops. The term is sometimes jocularly used in an adult context with much the same meaning.

plonk A casual term for alcoholic drink, usually wine, used by New Zealand and Australian soldiers during the Second World War, as a corruption of the French *vin blanc*.

Plunket A system of support for mothers and babies, with advice on feeding, medical checks, weighing and so on. Incorporated in February 1908 as the Society for the Promotion of the Health of Women and Children, the organisation soon became known as the Plunket Society, after Lady Victoria Plunket, wife of the then Governor of New Zealand, who took a great interest in its work. The Plunket Society was well organised, and branches were established nationwide (known as Plunket rooms). Long after the Plunkets left New Zealand their name lived on in such terms as Plunket nurse (specialising in the care of mothers and babies), Plunket baby (babies brought up under the advice of the Society) and Plunket book (the written record of a baby's growth and progress).

plurry A corruption of 'bloody' developed by Maori during the 19th century.
(See **py korry**)

pluty *abbrev.* of plutocrat, referring to a lifestyle that shows evidence of wealth, social advantage, or cultural and living habits often considered more refined, and possibly inaccessible, to those of less economic stability.

pohutukawa *Maori* A large native coast-growing tree, of spectacular gnarled growth, familiar in the northern areas of New Zealand, *Metrosideros excelsa*. Maori historically used juice from its inner bark for medicinal purposes (healing wounds, curing toothache and calming inflammation). By the mid-19th century pohutukawa timber was being extensively used for the ribs of sailing ships, and proved very serviceable in salt water. In December the tree produces bunches of bright red flowers, causing it to be known as the New Zealand Christmas tree. According to traditional Maori belief, the pohutukawa tree at Cape Reinga, the northernmost tip of the North Island, is many centuries old. It is sacred to Maori, who regard it as the departure point for the spirits of the dead, who are leaving for the next world.

poi *Maori* A small ball made of dried bulrush fluff bound together with long strips of dried leaves and suspended on a string. In earlier times the word was sometimes spelt poe, and was used by both males and females, but today only women swing poi in very decorative and complex patterns, on either short or long strings. Today poi are often made of rolled-up crushed plastic bags, appropriately decorated. Americans familiar with Hawaii are sometimes confused by the word's meaning in New Zealand, since poi in Hawaii is a kind of heavy starch pudding made from roots.

poked Exhausted. The imagery appears to stem from tiredness after sex.

poke the borax To make fun of, or demean. The term has nothing to do with hydrated disodium tetraborate (borax), but is derived from the Australian native dialect of Wathawurung, in which the word *borak* means no, not, or nonsense. This was adopted by white Australians as a form of put-down.

pokie *abbrev.* of poker machine – a gambling device operated with coins, the name is borrowed from the card game of poker.

polly, poly (1) Informal *abbrev.* of politician. (2) Informal *abbrev.* of Polynesian.

Polynesia(n) The area of the Pacific that includes Hawaii, Samoa, Easter Island, Tonga, New Zealand, Tahiti, Niue, the Cook Islands and Tokelau, and all peoples native to that area. The word is Greek and means 'many islands'. The local New Zealand Polynesian race is called Maori, who can be differentiated by calling the others Pacific Islanders. But sometimes Polynesian is substituted for Pacific Islanders, even though Maori *are* Polynesians.

Pom, Pommy An informal term referring to a person born or raised in the British Isles. The history of the term has been open to much dispute. Language expert Eric Partridge is firm in the belief that pommy is an abbreviation of pomegranate, related to the echoic phrase Jimmy Grant – a rhyming trick, which meant immigrant. In the second half of the 20th century, a certain distaste for British ways caused pommy to be very frequently associated with the word whingeing (complaining) and/or bastard. Pom and pommy have become somewhat imaginatively extended over the years, so fanciful developments are sometimes heard: Pom-land, Pomgolia and sometimes Pongolia, all slang terms for England.

poncy Precious in their manner, showy with money, or snobbish in their associations. The word was originally related to the French and Spanish words for prostitute. It has always had a connotation of ostentatious or pretentious behaviour, but in Britain also carries a side-meaning of probably being involved as a pimp for ladies of the night. The latter connotation is completely absent in New Zealand.

ponga *Maori* A tree fern, *Cyathea dealbata*, with characteristic silver-backed leaves – giving New Zealand its affiliation with the name and image of silver fern. It is sometimes misspelled as punga.

poozle The salvaging of useable or attractive goods from abandoned properties or other people's castoff rubbish. The word is used elsewhere – an old slang term for female genitalia, and a weird alien character in *Doctor Who* – but its

New Zealand application is not known to bear any relation to either of these.

pop Making a movement that is quick and easy. You pop a piece of bacon under a grill, pop a dish into the oven, etc. Socially, to pop in describes an informal, probably brief, visit. To pop over means to visit soon and to pop back means to return later. To pop off can mean to leave somewhere fairly abruptly, or – to die.

porangi *Maori* Behaving in a manner outside that which is normally accepted, mentally unbalanced.

poroporoaki *Maori* A ritual farewell ceremony with speeches.

possum *abbrev.* for **opossum** Australian opossums were released in New Zealand in 1837, by Captain John Howell at Riverton in Southland. During the 19th century further releases took place, with the idea that the animals might multiply and provide the basis for a fur industry. Multiply they did: a century later, opossums in New Zealand outnumbered sheep and people. They also destroyed vast numbers of trees and carried cattle tuberculosis. Their fur never became a major industry: they are a pugnacious animal and their skins often have scars and holes, besides varying in colour through differing regional diets, making the pelts difficult to match. But developments in bleaching, dyeing and mixing the detached fur with fine quality wool have resulted in a re-positioning of opossum as a now-desirable element within the clothing (if not fur) industry.

The name comes from a native American word for the animal. While opossum is sometimes heard in a formal context, public usage invariably prefers the abbreviated form, possum.

'Pot,' the The star group formally known as the Belt of Orion, a grouping which stands out brightly in the night sky.

New Zealanders call this the Pot because that is what it looks like: a squarish group of bright spots with a fifth, the handle, to one side. It rises in the east every night, tracks across the sky in patterns according to the season and always sets in the west.

Australians sometimes call it the Saucepan. It should not to be confused with a similar American habit of calling Sagittarius the Teapot.

pot, to Reporting, sometimes clandestinely, a misdemeanour that has hitherto been unnoticed but which, as a result of the information, becomes a focus of attention. It is sometimes used in the sense of being a betrayal, but also occasionally more formally when seen as advancing the common good. The image may come from the action of placing someone in a pot from which there is little chance of escape, or as an abbreviation of put someone's pot on, which carries the idea of uncomfortable heat generated beneath them.
(See **dob in**)

potae *Maori* A hat.

potterati A fanciful created word applied to those groups of people who lead what is perceived as an arty lifestyle, and may be versed in the skills of weaving, herb gardens, yoga – and pottery.

pottle A small and insubstantial container, meant to hold a portion of berry fruits, or other foods, sometimes moist, such as yoghurt or fruit salad.
(See **chip, punnet**)

pounamu *Maori* See **greenstone**

power cut Cessation of electricity supply, sometimes notified (for reasons of repair or major alteration in services), sometimes not (by emergency or accident).
(See **outage**)

powhiri *Maori* A formal Maori welcome, involving careful placing of the hosts on one side of an invisible line, and the visitors or manuhiri on the other side. Alternating representatives from each side make speeches, and it is imperative that each be rounded off with a song or waiata, either from the speaker themselves, or a representative (who is a better singer) or the entire group. When all the speakers and songs reach a conclusion, the visitors advance over the invisible line and are greeted individually, usually with a hongi, by the hosts. The visitors then have a 'place for their feet' on the hosts' territory.
(See **mihi, hongi, poroporoaki, wero**)

preventive detention Commitment to prison, usually for sexual offences or serious violence, of offenders over 18 who are considered likely to commit further offences. Imprisonment can be of indefinite length but has a minimum of five years.

pricker, to get on someone's Irritation caused by either a person or a situation, often arising because of some repetition of the initial irritating occurrence, which can eventually reach actual anger. The image arises from the similar irritation of plant prickles. *The woman next to me at work sniffs all day, and the sound really gets on my pricker.*

procesh *abbrev.* of procession. The word is often used by university students to refer to a passage through the city on foot as part of the annual graduation ceremonies.

puha *Maori* A leafy green weed otherwise known as sow thistle, much favoured as a Maori vegetable, and often served cooked, to accompany pork.

pukana *Maori* A distorted facial expression involving noticeably enlarging the eyes and projecting the tongue, traditionally aimed at demonstrating fierceness and power but occasionally also to amuse. The assumed wide stare is believed to be influenced by an intention to resemble the wisdom of an owl.

pukeko *Maori* A swamp bird, *Porphyrio melanotus*, approximately the size of a full-grown hen, blackish-purple in colour, with a red beak, long red legs and a jaunty tail that constantly flicks up the white feathers underneath. Sometimes known just as a puke, pronounced *pook*, the pukeko is common even in cities when roads run near water. An old joke says that to cook a pukeko, you pluck and draw the bird, place it in a pot together with a stone, boil it gently for some three hours – then eat the stone.

puku *Maori* Stomach. In the Maori language its literal meaning is a swelling. When used in English the word has a connotation that the stomach referred to is big, but slim people, and even young children, can say that they have a full puku after a meal.

pull a fast one The successful execution of a deception. *The man claimed a sickness benefit, but had pulled a fast one to get it: he faked the doctor's signature.*
(See **quickie, swiftie**)

punnet See **chip, pottle**

puriri *Maori* A tall native tree (*Vitex lucens*) with prolific, slightly crinkly leaves and soft flowers which produce berries that attract many birds, hence the occasionally heard name, food tree.

putiputi *Maori* A flower.

py korry A Maori version of by golly, which is an innocuous version of by God. Maori adopted the phrase into their own language as py korry.
(See **plurry**)

Q

Queen's Birthday The first Monday in June is a public holiday, celebrating the official birthday of the Queen of New Zealand. The custom dates back to 1910, when King George V came to the throne in Britain. His birthday was on 3 June, in (British) mid-summer, and the celebration of his birthday became an established public holiday.

Queen Street farmer An urban business person who owns a farm property as a financial proposition. The term, which has derogatory connotations, dates from the 1950s and refers to Auckland's main commercial street. Also sometimes heard is the Wellington version, Featherston Street farmer. *I don't know who owns the property now – Joe sold it to a Queen Street farmer.*

quickie (1) A brief bout of sex, or some alcoholic drinking of short duration. (2) A deception, a trick, a successful subterfuge, carried out swiftly and confidently – along the lines of the quickness of the hand deceiving the eye.
(See **swiftie**)

quiet, on the Secretly, discreetly, either for clandestine reasons or out of discretion and modesty. Sometimes abbreviated to on the q.t.

R

raddle A thick, heavy piece of coloured chalk used to mark livestock for identification assistance when drafting. The word began in old English as *rudd*, meaning red, and because the most common marker used by farmers was made from an ochre, which was red, by the 1500s the chalk was called ruddle, which gradually became raddle. These days, raddle, which may also be blue, yellow or green, comes in a spray can.

rahui *Maori* A ritual decree issued by a Maori community leader, which prohibits specified activities in a nominated area for a prescribed period, often because of a death in the area. For example, a drowning may result in the prohibition of fishing, shellfish gathering and swimming in the area until the rahui is lifted. Such a decree can also be modified to forbid a prescribed activity, considered disadvantageous to the community, e.g. using illegal drugs.

ranchslider A sliding glass door, often of generous height, dividing the interior of a house from a deck or patio.

rangatira *Maori* An important person, usually of chiefly rank, a leader.

rangatiratanga *Maori* The concept of chiefly rule, frequently interpreted as Maori governing their own activities independently of any other influences or obligations.

rata *Maori* A tree (*Metrosideros robusta*) and also a vine (*Metrosideros fulgens*), both characterised by beautiful red brush-like flowers.

Ratana *Maori* A religious and political movement established by Tahupotiki Wiremu Ratana after the First World War. A mystic with great belief in faith healing, Ratana placed himself at the centre, as the instrument of God. Ratana was unassuming and modest, but also a commanding and influential figure among his Maori followers. He considered most ritual as meaningless and discouraged medical treatment. The Ratana church has traditionally been allied with the Labour Party.

ratbag A distasteful person, considered worthless and probably unreliable and underhand. The term is believed to have developed from 19th-century rat catchers who literally carried a bag into which they put captured rats.

rat on To turn away from an established loyalty and betray, to reveal a confidence. Often used in connection with conveying information to an authority such as the police about activities which the participants would prefer to have kept discreet.
(See **dob**)

rattle your dags A request or command to move faster, to hurry. When sheep have lumps of dry dung hanging off their rear end and they are moving fast, the dry lumps actually do rattle. *Raewyn was still dithering round, and I could see the bus coming down the street, so I yelled at her that if she didn't rattle her dags, we'd miss it!*
(See **dag**)

rat up a drainpipe, like a Very fast. The expression is often applied to fast movement into slightly questionable activity, such as eating voraciously, quickly understanding some illegal or underhand activity, or taking advantage of sexual opportunity. *When the pretty new neighbour asked Arnie if he'd come inside and help her with a broken shelf, he was in there like a rat up a drainpipe.*

raupo *Maori* A tall swamp-growing shrub (*Typha augustifolia*) with upright stems of tiny flowers, which produce copious pollen. Before the arrival of Europeans this pollen was collected, mixed with fluid and baked into cakes. The seed-heads when dry give the plant a characteristic profile, and their fluffy nature is ideal for stuffing the inside of poi. Elsewhere the plant is known as a bulrush.

real estate Land, both urban or rural. Originating in the Latin *res*, meaning 'thing', real estate generally refers to property which is immovable – it exists but cannot be carried away. Those who sell real estate are called estate agents; in the United States they are realtors who sell realty.

rego *abbrev.* of car registration.

regular (1) At equal intervals: *There is a regular bus service from this stop* or *He always arrives on Tuesday – as regular as clockwork*. The word is derived from the Latin *regula*, meaning a ruler. (2) Normal, ordinary, or medium-sized. This American-based usage appears to be related to by-passing the word 'small' so that many fast food outlets offer items which are large or regular.

Reinga *Maori* Te Reinga or Cape Reinga is the northernmost tip of New Zealand. Its most famous inhabitant is an ancient pohutukawa tree which figures prominently in Maori legends of death. These describe how, immediately after death, the spirit of a Maori person travels north until it reaches Reinga, upon which it descends on the roots of the pohutukawa tree into the ocean depths. It then emerges some distance away, for a farewell view of the land of the living, before proceeding to the other world. Reinga means leaping place.

rellies *abbrev.* of relatives, within the custom of baby-talk abbreviations.

Remuera tractor (aka **Fendalton tractor**) A scornful name for heavy-duty four-wheel drive vehicles which tend to be favoured by upper-income people for solely urban use. Remuera is a well-heeled Auckland suburb; Fendalton is its Christchurch equivalent.

reo, te *Maori* Language. Basically te reo means voice or speech but is usually used to mean language – and most specifically the Maori language. An adjective is sometimes added so that te reo Pakeha would mean the English language. But used unadorned, te reo usually indicates the Maori language.

reserve An area of publicly owned land set aside for recreation, usually, but not necessarily, in an urban setting. It may be large enough to contain sports facilities, or just a quite small grassy area. A reserve is not usually large enough to be called a park. (See **domain**)

resource consent Official approval for a landowner to alter land in some way, such as burning, allowing the discharge of contamination or subdividing it into housing habitation sections. Authorisation is issued under the Resource Management Act, which protects the physical and natural properties of the country and the actions of humans in relation to the natural environment.

retread A tyre whose road-gripping surface has become worn out, and has been replaced with a new notched surface. The image is sometimes transferred to people who have moved to a slightly different version of a former career or have returned to work after retiring. *After that nasty appendicitis operation Mary seems to have a new lease on life and her career has had a retread.*

reverse To drive a car backwards. This simple term can confuse those from other countries, who tend to say back up.

rewarewa *Maori* A large forest tree (*Knightia excelsa*) with notch-edged leaves and a timber with an attractively patterned grain, often found in fine quality cabinetmaking.

rewena *Maori* A transliteration of leaven.
(See **Maori bread**)

right as rain Affirmation that everything is going well, the speaker is confident of a good outcome and needs no further assistance. The expression right as something has been in English since medieval times, using a string of comparatives, such as trivet or ninepence. Right as rain emerged in the 19th century and took precedence over all the previous forms, possibly because of its pleasing alliteration, and also possibly because rain is perceived as good, and causes growth. *When the plaster came off, she stumbled around with a stick but after a week she was walking as right as rain.*

right-o, right-ho, righty-o An emphatic agreement, a signal of certainty. While 'right' on its own might be sufficient to indicate approval, 'oh' acts as an intensifier.

rimu *Maori* A forest tree (*Dacrydium cupressinum*) with filament-shaped foliage and an overall 'droopy' outline. It grows prolifically, and to considerable height, with timber which is much prized for its attractiveness and durability. Rimu is sometimes called red pine.

Ringatu *Maori* A Maori religious movement founded by Te Kooti Arikirangi Te Turuki, who, while imprisoned on the Chatham Islands in the 1860s, evolved a gentle and dignified version of Christian faith, with no public demonstration, robes or stipendiary clergy. The faith lasted long after the death of Te Kooti in 1893.

ringbark A practice by which a tree is killed when its bark is cut deeply right around the trunk's perimeter. The word is sometimes used to describe a person whose effectiveness is decreasing, as if their sap is no longer rising.

ringer A highly skilled sheep shearer, the fastest in the shearing shed. The term may have its origin in a British dialect word for excellent, first-class, but is believed to have been used by 19th-century Australian shearers with the meaning that their leader's shearing technique could run rings around anyone else's.

ring up To make a phone call. To use a phone in New Zealand in the early days, you had to vigorously turn a handle to create a ring that alerted the operator or to alert other callers on a shared party line. This led to the phrase 'to ring someone' or to 'ring them up'. The expression is still used, often in preference to 'I'll call', which in New Zealand tends to mean 'I'll visit'.

rip, shit and bust To act with concentrated energy, without finesse and without consideration for any possible consequences. The venture may earn as much disapproval because of the mayhem in its wake, as approval for its eventual success. *When she asked him to clear the section he hoed into it, rip shit and bust, but made a worse mess.*

Roaring Meg A South Island stream, 15 kilometres from Cromwell in Otago. Four differing legends provide origins for the name, each involving a woman, either tempestuous, frightened, voluble or complaining. Nobody will ever know which, if any, is true.
(See **Gentle Annie**)

Rogernomics The fiscal revolution brought about by Sir Roger Douglas, New Zealand's Minister of Finance from 1984 to 1988. He introduced a new goods and services tax and privatised much of the state sector, bringing to an end government control of such areas as postal services and railways. The term Rogernomics was first noticed in print in 1985.

rohe *Maori* A tribal boundary, and the area within the boundary.

RONZ *abbrev.* for the Rest of New Zealand, an ironic label for that part of the country and its population which lie south of

the Bombay Hills (an area perceived as being the outer limit of Greater Auckland).
(See **JAFA, Bombay Hills**)

root   Slang term for sexual intercourse.

rooted   Tired out and unable to continue. The term is based on a perception of post-coital weariness, but can also be applied to non-human situations: a machine or mechanical system which is malfunctioning or has failed completely could be described as rooted. *The old car broke down on the first steep hill – the engine was absolutely rooted.*

ropeable   Very angry indeed, almost requiring restraint, akin to fit to be tied.

ropey   Not well organised, unreliable, of doubtful efficiency, and possibly also smelly. The image comes from a bacterial infection in beer, which develops slimy threads throughout the liquid and renders it useless. *Evan suggested investing some money in a franchise hamburger bar, but I thought the financial structure was a bit ropey.*

Rotovegas   An amusing and affectionate nickname for Rotorua, combining its name with Las Vegas, as a none-too-subtle acknowledgement of the tourist and Maori entertainment industry that makes up a major part of the local economy.

rough as guts   Lacking polish – not necessarily lacking value, but available only in a form free of restraint or refinement. Variations on 'rough' as comparisons have been in use for over a century: as bags, as a badger's behind, as a goat's knees, as a pig's breakfast. Rough as guts has won particular affection, since it can be a criticism and a pejorative, but not always: it may describe someone who is a rough diamond but who can deliver what is required. *When Jamie cooks dinner, he produces a spectacular meal, though* *if you saw him at work in the kitchen you'd think he was as rough as guts.*

rua *Maori* (1) The number two. (2) A prolific and well-known breed of potato. (3) A hole or pit, which can be either a storing place for dried foods, or a grave.

rubber The stretchy substance resulting from dried plant latex. New Zealanders use the word in all its usual extended meanings – a division of a bridge game, a cheque that isn't honoured, a thin band used to hold a roll of papers, a stamp, a person who gapes inquisitively (rubbernecker) – but one customary use sometimes requires explanation. In New Zealand a rubber is usually a pencil eraser, whereas for Australians and Americans it is a euphemism for a condom. The latter meaning is becoming more common in New Zealand: a recent safe sex campaign for young people used the word in that context.

rubbish tin A receptacle for unwanted material. It can be big enough to hold all the waste from a household or a building, or as small as a lift-top container known as a kitchen tidy. The same receptacle in other cultures might be called a trash can or garbage bin.

runanga *Maori* A meeting or organisation which assembles for administrative purposes, a council. Extra words can outline what kind of runanga is being referred to: a runanga-a-iwi is a meeting of tribal members; a whare runanga is the meeting house in which deliberations are carried out.

S

Sa *abbrev.* for Samoan, often used casually among themselves by Samoans living in New Zealand and not considered offensive when said to them by non-Samoans.

sammie *abbrev.* of sandwich (maintaining the local speech characteristic of using childish abbreviations). Although John Montagu, Earl of Sandwich did not invent sandwiches – the Romans had eaten something similar hundreds of years before – the English language certainly named them after him, when, unwilling to leave the gambling tables for 24 hours at a stretch, he ate meat-between-bread with one hand while he gambled with the other.

sandshoe A lightweight canvas shoe, usually white, with a rubber sole, and worn for beachwear, tennis and casual occasions. An alternative name is sneaker. The British word plimsoll has never won acceptance in New Zealand. A traditional sandshoe is different from the American-influenced trainer, which is sometimes ankle high, with such features as air-pocket soles and netting inserts. The trainer was originally a running shoe, but its new name has helped make it a popular item of footwear. Sandshoe and sneaker are now seldom used in New Zealand.

sausages Both those linked in a string and those from which chunks are cut. In some places overseas, the former are known as links. In New Zealand sausages are also known as snags (from the Lancashire word *snackles*, meaning small morsels of food), snarlers (from the military, where some thought the noise of frying sausages sounded like dogs snarling) and bangers (also military on the same lines).
(See **banger** and **cheerio**)

sausage sizzle Outdoor cooking, barbecue-style, of sausages, usually served with onion and/or tomato sauce in a slice of bread. This is a favourite way of raising funds for sporting, school or charity events, often by mounting the sizzle in a public place such as a shopping centre.

scarfie Informal name for university students, particularly those at the University of Otago in Dunedin. Woollen scarves, sometimes in the university colours and sometimes not, are a necessity in chilly Dunedin winters, but the students' fondness for wearing their scarves in other seasons as well led to the term scarfie. The expression is fairly regional in use but most New Zealanders are now familiar with it, especially since the Robert Sarkies film, *Scarfies*.

scone A lightweight dough-cake, cooked in an oven or sometimes on a griddle and occasionally containing raisins or dates. To be excellent, scones must be home-made and fresh. To Americans scones are usually baking powder biscuits. Scone is thought to come from an old German word *schoonbrot* (fine bread). New Zealanders pronounce the word *sconn*.

scone, loaf, bun The head. A group of scone expressions has developed directly out of the slang meaning of head. To use your scone means to think carefully; to be off your scone is to be functioning abnormally; to do your scone (or your bun) means to express marked anger. Loaf is from the rhyming slang loaf of bread, head. Bun may have developed from that association, also to mean head.

Scots(man's) grandstand A home-made structure on private property which allows a view of an outdoor events centre, thus able to accommodate people for watching a race meeting, athletic event or concert without paying admission.

scroggin A home-made and easily carried high-energy snack food favoured by trampers and bushwalkers. The name is thought to come from the initial letters of the traditional ingredients: sultanas, chocolate, raisins, orange peel (candied), ginger (crystallised), glucose barley sugar, imagination and nuts. Scroggin is sometimes known as trail mix.

scrub Low, stunted vegetation often growing in sub-standard soil, also an area covered in this kind of growth. New Zealanders often talk about scrub-cutting, which refers to the clearing of such plants. The word has long been a slang term for a contemptible person, invariably male, which is probably why the plant variety is usually regarded as unimpressive and stunted. The word is not related to the term scrubber, however, which is an old military word for a lowly woman, usually with loose morals.

scunge Accumulated dirt, grease or detritus, or a person decreed to be despicable by the speaker. Often heard as the adjective, scungy, which can describe something unsavoury such as a dirty bath or an untidy kitchen.

sealed road (tar-sealed) Surfaced with tar macadam, asphalt, bituminous pitch – as opposed to unsealed.
(See **asphalt, metal**)

section A piece of land cut off from a greater piece, or each piece of a considerable division. In New Zealand the word usually describes the piece of land on which a house is situated. Americans call their own piece of domestic land the yard and what New Zealanders would call an empty section is to Americans a vacant lot.

set (against), have a A firmly held negative opinion concerning a person, plan, activity or philosophy, sometimes, but not always, without any logical basis. It can be intensified as dead set against.

shagroon An archaic name for settlers from Australia, especially those who were not able to afford land ownership. The word was common during the 19th century. Shagroon is possibly descended from Gaelic *seachran* meaning wanderer and the English version has been spelt various ways. It was used principally in the Canterbury area and had a decidedly derogatory resonance.

Shaky Isles Because it is prone to earthquakes, New Zealand is sometimes called the Shaky Isles, especially by Australians. Ironically, Australia actually has more earthquakes than New Zealand.

shanghai A forked stick with an elastic strip fitted across the fork, used mainly by boys as a device for firing small missiles in fun or in attack. The word derives from the Scottish dialect word *shangan*, meaning a stick with a cleft in its end, sometimes used for clipping messages to a dog's tail. Nineteenth-century non-Scottish New Zealanders, hearing the word *shangan* (sometimes shangy) were unconsciously influenced by the name of the Chinese city, Shanghai. By 1884 in New Zealand shanghai had acquired its present meaning. A shanghai is known elsewhere as a catapult.

share-milker A worker on a dairy farm who, by agreement with the owner, receives a proportion of the farm's income in return for labour and involvement. There are many variations on this farming style, which has been the backbone of the New Zealand dairying industry. The word has been used in New Zealand since the early 1900s.

sheila An informal word for a (usually) young woman. Sheila is an Irish name derived from an old Celtic name. Since the early 1830s it has been used in Britain as a slang term for a woman, and surfaced in New Zealand about 1900 with the same meaning. Originally somewhat disrespectful, the word is now used in a much more user-friendly way, as a feminine equivalent of bloke. A recent film documentary about feminism in New Zealand, made by a woman, was called *Sheilas 28 Years On*.

she'll be right Everything will be fine, there will be a happy outcome. 'She' is used here in an abstract, non-feminine sense for inanimate concepts: it can refer to the current situation, the weather, a vehicle – anything.
(See **jake, she'll be**)

sherang See **head sherang**

shiack, shyack, chiack High-spirited, non-destructive and cheerful activity. The origin of the word is the Cockney term *chi-hike*, which meant teasing and making impertinent remarks. In New Zealand the word is far more often used to describe the physical boisterousness of young men.

shicker, shickered Drunk. Adapted from the Hebrew *shikor*, which became the Yiddish *skikker* (drunk), the word was learnt by Cockneys in London from Jewish immigrants during the late 19th century.

shingle short Reduced mental ability, from the image of an incomplete roof, lacking several tiles.
(See **kumara short of a hangi**)

shitty, throw a An explosion of anger, a temperamental outburst. The expression is created from the not unreasonable assumption that, since shit is unpleasant, it can be invoked to describe anything else unpleasant.

shoot through To depart, often in haste and sometimes without explanation or farewells.

shorts *abbrev.* for short pants. There are various styles of shorts: in the mid- to late 20th century many New Zealand men wore what were known as walkshorts, semi-formal garments made of heavy fabric and worn with long socks; elastic-waisted lightweights are known as boxer shorts and worn as underpants. In the United States shorts are usually underpants.

In New Zealand shorts can also mean the promotions, commercials and trailers shown at a cinema before the main feature.
(See **trailer**)

shout   To pay for someone else. It is believed to be an old form of the English word shot, meaning charge or payment: to stand shot meant to pay the bill. Also relevant is the noisiness of an English inn, and later Australian gold-digging bars, where you had to shout at the publican to order a drink for yourself and your friends. When, in 2005, the major New Zealand beer company Dominion Breweries celebrated their 75 years in business by inviting all adults in New Zealand to enjoy a free beer, the promotion was titled 'Shout the Nation'. Americans do not shout in this way: they host or treat.
(See **Parnell shout**)

shower   A gift-giving social occasion held, usually by women, to celebrate an engagement or marriage, or the birth of a baby. The idea is based on the once-necessary custom of a bride taking a dowry to her marriage. The legend about a shower replacing a dowry is said to have originated in old Holland, when a kind miller gave away so much bread to the poor that he could not afford to marry the girl he loved – until those to whom he had been a benefactor showered the young woman with simple household gifts so the young couple were able to marry.

shufty, (shifty), have a   A look, a brief examination. The word originated as military slang among British servicemen based in the Middle East, and is derived from the Arabic term *sufti*, meaning Have you seen? *After taking a quick shufty though a small gap in the curtain, Miriam told the stage manager that the audience was all seated.*

sickie, to throw a   Informal term describing time away from employment because of illness – sick leave. Since such leave is sometimes applied for in less than genuine circumstances, the term can have a slightly ironic resonance. *It seemed a bit of a coincidence that Benjamin threw a sickie on Monday when he'd been up north for his brother's wedding on Saturday.*

silence, two minutes' A reverent custom observed on solemn ritual occasions around the world, the term has been adapted in New Zealand to indicate that a short silence is required for some other purpose – most commonly reading a small local newspaper.

silly as a chook, wet hen, two bob watch A succession of nonsense similes based on the perceived eccentricity of the items named. Domestic hens have small heads and behaviour which often seems irrational, so the term silly as a chook indicates whimsicality and probable lack of intelligence. And hens, when wet, become distressed and disorientated. A two bob watch refers back to pre-decimal currency when a watch bought for 2 shillings (20 cents) was not expected to last for very long.

silver beet New Zealand name for the rich green leafy vegetable known elsewhere as spinach beet or Swiss chard. The name, used in New Zealand since about 1900, is believed to come from the wide, silvery-white central stalk.

silver fern A national symbol for New Zealand, especially in relation to sports teams. The beautiful silver fern was a common emblem of New Zealand before the kiwi. The country was sometimes called Fernland; the Native Rugby Team used it as an emblem when touring Britain in 1888 and the 1905 the All Blacks did the same; after 1900 it appeared on New Zealand's meat and dairy exports; First World War New Zealand servicemen were commonly known or Fernleaves and in the Second World War as Silver Ferns. In 1990, this last name was given to the New Zealand representative netball players. The New Zealand Rugby Union has copyrighted the silver fern frond, which is used as the All Black symbol.

singlet Men's undershirt, usually sleeveless, but also worn by women as a fashion item. The name originates from an ancient design of top garment worn by men in Europe, featuring a fairly tight top with sleeves and a little skirt. These varied a great deal, but because they always had an outer layer of fabric and an inner layer of lining, they were called a doublet (i.e. two layers of fabric). During the 18th century, some upper garments for men began to be made with only one layer of fabric. These floppier garments came to be worn underneath rather than on top and usually had no sleeves and no lining. This undergarment became known as a singlet.

Singlets then developed styles of their own, sometimes with sleeves, sometimes without (athletic singlets) and long-sleeved singlets (called spencers, named after an ancestor of the late Princess Diana). The word is virtually unknown in the United States, where undershirt is much more common. A singlet made of black wool, often worn by New Zealand workmen, is commonly called a bush singlet.

sink (a few) To have some (alcoholic) drinks at leisure, usually involving groups of males only.

sinking lid An informal description of a Government policy whereby staff numbers in certain departments are slowly reduced, by not bringing in any new personnel to replace those who leave their positions, or die.

sitting up like Jacky In a prominent position and easily seen. Early Australians referred to any Aboriginal as Jacky (which was comparable with Hori in New Zealand) and the phrase developed because Aboriginals stood out among white workers.

skint *abbrev.* of skinned, signifying metaphorical nakedness – without any funds.

skite *abbrev.* of the old British word blatherskite, meaning a noisy, talkative, silly person. More recently, Australians and New Zealanders have shortened the word to skite, and the meaning has altered a little to mean a person who annoys others by boasting or showing off.

skitters, squitters   (1) Diarrhoea. (2) State of nervousness (as in skittish, meaning capricious, whimsical, irresponsible).

skull, scull   To drink alcohol, especially quickly, and often as a whole glass without pause. The word derives from a corruption of the Scandinavian drinking toast *skol* from *skaal*, bowl, now signifying good health, cheers.

slab   Two dozen bottles (or cans) of beer, packed into one carton. The term is widely used in Australia, but understood in New Zealand.

slather, open   (1) Easily able to be approached or to participate in, open to all comers, free for all. The derivation is obscure, but is believed to be related to an old Irish word meaning access. (2) Without open, slather also retains the meaning more common in the United States and Canada of a large amount, e.g. to slather copious butter and jam on bread. (3) A British use of slather, meaning to thrash, is seldom heard in New Zealand.

slinter, to pull a, to work a   A devious manipulation, a trick, a deception, something slightly underhand organised to be advantageous to the person who instigates it. The term came into English during the First World War, and may have originated from a Dutch word that moved into Afrikaans as *schlenter*, meaning not genuine, counterfeit, of doubtful integrity. Phrases containing slinter have been commonly used in New Zealand since 1864.

slippers   Soft-soled shoes for wearing inside the house. In some places, such as Honolulu, slippers means jandals, which can be confusing for visiting New Zealanders. In the United States, slippers are commonly referred to as mules.

sly grog Selling liquor illegally and by necessity clandestinely, either during times or days when alcohol sale is forbidden, or from premises that are not licensed to sell alcohol at all. The term, now obsolete, was in wide use during the period when liquor could be sold only by establishments that also offered accommodation and all alcohol sales ceased at 6 p.m.

smoko A short break in performing a long task, or a break at a regular time of day, in a full-time job. Back in the 19th century workers used to look forward to regular breaks when they could have a smoke, which was signalled by someone calling out 'smoke oh' or 'smoke ho', and gradually the word became smoko. Now it applies to any break, whether smoking is involved or not.

snags See **sausages**

snarky Contrived combination of sarcastic and nasty.

snarlers See **sausages**

sneaker See **sandshoe**

snib A moveable button or knob on the inside portion of a Yale-type door lock. When it is slid into a certain position, it prevents the door being opened from the outside with the key, or from the inside with the handle.

snitch (1) A dislike for a person, place or plan, sometimes without logical reason. You can also take a snitcher against someone. (2) An informer, one who reveals otherwise confidential information. (3) To steal (rare).

snort A casual and informal term for an alcoholic drink.

solicitor A lawyer. Some other countries call lawyers attorneys and for them solicitors are people who are asking for something, like con men, prostitutes and beggars, who pester you.

sook A person lacking courage, unwilling and of weak temperament – though possibly used only as a specific gibe. The word is derived from suck, as in a breast-feeding infant.

sool An instruction given to a dog to chase or attack other animals or something dangerous. The derivation is an interesting reversal: it comes from an old English word *sowl*, meaning to grasp a dog and temporarily disable it. Sool is often followed by on.

southern man A term referring to men living, and preferably born in, the South Island, with connotations of taciturnity, reliability, masculinity and a liking for wide open spaces. The expression probably arose as the North Island became more populous and urban, creating a certain disdain in the south, which sees itself as closer to the 'real' New Zealand. The southern man idea provides the basis for a popular series of TV and billboard commercials for Speight's beer. There was a mild *frisson* when it was revealed that actors hired for the campaign were actually from Auckland and Australia.

spacies A general term for the video games played in amusement parlours, generally by young people. The name is derived from an abbreviation of the early examples called Space Invaders.

sparkie Informal term for a professional electrician.

spaz Applied to a person who appears to be out of control. It is an insensitive abbreviation of spastic.

spine bashing Lying down comfortably. A jocular term of military origin, it indicates a complete absence of activity in contrast to strenuous periods of marching or square bashing.

spit the dummy Be very angry, lose one's temper. The term comes from the noise made by a baby who spits out a dummy or rubber teat and cries loudly. Originally an Australian expression, it is usually pejorative – the person so described is perhaps rather querulous. *When Mel saw the new roster she spat the dummy and refused to work the new hours.*

spot ya An informal and very reduced way of saying 'I look forward to meeting you again sometime later', another version of 'see you'.

sprog A baby, child, or very young person. The term was originally used in branches of the military early in the Second World War, referring to new recruits. It may be a corruption of a very old English word *sprag*, whose meaning was a twig broken from a plant – hence something young and green. Later a sprog came to be applied to a young man, especially a lively one. From there it was used to describe a youth raw to military life, but by 1945 the word was being commonly applied to a baby.

squiz An analytical examination, a look – possibly quick, but careful. It is a combination of quiz and squint. *We were late for the viewing but Emmy had time for a quick squiz at the kitchen and decided that the house wouldn't do.*

stairdancer A thief who moves adroitly up and down multi-storey buildings, stealing from offices and escaping via the staircase. The word came into use in New Zealand during the early 1950s.

stand (1) A group of trees. Known elsewhere as a copse, coppice or spinney. (2) Tiered seating for watching a big event, sports match or concert, correctly called a grandstand but often referred to as just a stand. (3) New Zealanders stand for political election (whereas Americans run for office). (4) Pedigree stud animals, especially horses, are said to stand at a certain address.

state house Houses built by the New Zealand government from the 1930s onwards in order to help people financially disadvantaged by the depression. The state owned the houses and charged only a modest rental. By 1950, 23,000 had been built. As the aspiration towards self-ownership of property increased, the government gradually offered state house tenants the chance to buy their homes, and made government loans available for private house building.

Steinie A bottle or can of beer, accurately that of the brand Steinlager, a 1963 trade name registered by New Zealand Breweries /Lion Breweries.

stickies An informal name for sweet dessert wines.

sticking plaster Strip of fabric with one side strongly adhesive and medicated, for protection of minor wounds. Elsewhere known as Band-aids or adhesive plasters.

sticks, the Areas distant from urban resources, the hinterland. The image arises from countryside devoid of roads and buildings, but supplied only with bushes and trees – sticks. *Sally had been a city girl all her life and found living in the sticks very grim.*
(See **backblocks**)

stickybeak A person who takes an overdeveloped interest in the doings of others and likes to offer unwelcome opinions and interference. *She's such a stickybeak – her curtains are always twitching when we have visitors.*

stiff cheese/hard cheese Being in an unfortunate position, having bad luck. Obviously, stiff or hard cheese implies poor quality. Also an influence was the British custom of using the Persian word *chiz* meaning the tops, the best (as in the big cheese), which gives the extra connotation that things could have been successful but, alas, are not.

stirrer *abbrev.* of shit-stirrer, a person who deliberately creates trouble. By 1900 shit could be used to mean trouble and unpleasantness and the phrase arose from that. More polite versions developed – such as stick-stirrer and brown-handled stirrer and the shorthand, stirrer.

stock (1) The total goods held within a business, for instance a shop. (2) The animals on a farm (hence stockyards and stock sales). For Americans stock is a business term, referring to shares. The word stock comes from the old English *stocc*, meaning the stump of a tree, and therefore something solid and dependable.

stoked To be energised, happy, surprised, cheerful, in some way fired up. The word is derived from stoke, as in adding fuel to and tending a fire or furnace. As the actual action of stoking fires became rarer, from the 1950s onward, the word stoked became more popular. *I'm really stoked that you've been chosen to play for the All Blacks.*

stone end The absolute finish. In this usage, 'stone' functions as 'dead' does in the expression dead end.

stonkered Unable to continue, through exhaustion, or frustrated by some development which prevents progress. The word comes from the game of marbles, where stonk meant the stake a player must hazard before playing. From this came the verb stonkered, meaning to be beaten or stymied. Popular with the armed forces, the term entered wide general New Zealand use after the Second World War. *I thought I could run the marathon, but halfway through I was stonkered and had to drop out.*

stoush A fight, either physical (usually a fist-fight) or metaphorical, sometimes called a barney. The word is related to the old British word *stashie*, meaning a quarrel or an uproar and came to New Zealand with the settlers, who generally spelled it stouch. By the early 1900s the word was spelled stoush. It is now also a verb (to stoush, to get stoushed)

and appears in other variations (a stousher or stoush artist – enthusiastic fighter). The meaning has softened a little, so that now a phrase like *a bit of a stoush* describes a vigorous argument.
(See **barney**)

strapped for cash Very low on available funds. There have been various legends about the term's origin, but language scholars tend to believe that strap is a corruption of the rural term strip – to wait until the principal milking has finished, then draw the very last drop of milk from each cow. Hence strapped for cash would originally have meant stripped of cash, absolutely empty.

stratum or strata title(s) Certain legal rights regarding various levels of the air space above a specified area, and sometimes also various levels below it.

strewth *abbrev.* of in God's truth. This is one of several terms that modify the names of God and Jesus into something less offensive (e.g. golly, gosh, gee, crikey etc.). In God's truth! was said in Britain for several centuries as an exclamation of surprise, wonder, or disbelief and gradually, by the 1800s, the three words became one.

strike, strike me pink Expression of astonishment. Either alone (strike!) or in combination with unexpected contrasts, the series of 'strike me' expressions all indicate extreme surprise. The origin appears to be literal: someone is sufficiently startled to imagine themselves struck by something they normally are not – handsome, pink, lucky or dead.

stroppy Either authoritative or dictatorial, depending on the speaker's opinion, having strong ideas and effective ways of accomplishing their own way of doing things. Used only since the 1950s, stroppy is thought to be a strange abbreviation of obstreperous. Another possible influence is the strop on which men used to sharpen their razors – a fairly unyielding strip of hard leather. *Bernadette's one stroppy sheila – she'll always get her own way if she can.*

stubbie (1) A short thick bottle, usually containing beer. (2) Outdoor cotton shorts for men.
(See **tinny, tube, shorts**)

stuff around, stuff up Useless activity, procrastination, time wasted with nothing to show for it. In those contexts it can substitute for muck around. The related term stuff up signifies that a process or situation has been spoilt and is no longer viable, to the frustration of those who are waiting for its fruition. *Merle was stuffing around for so long that we were late for the concert.*
(See **muck around**)

stunned mullet A description of someone rendered inactive by surprise or shock. The image is of a fish that has been clubbed into insensibility. *When he found that he'd won ten thousand dollars, Roy's first reaction was just to sit there like a stunned mullet.*

sulky A lightly built two-wheeled conveyance drawn by a horse during harness racing or the trots, as it is sometimes known.

super (1) *abbrev.* for New Zealand superannuation, the small fortnightly government payment made to all people over 65 since 1898 and originally called the old age pension. Someone who receives super is a superannuitant. (2) *abbrev.* of superphosphate, a fertiliser spread on New Zealand farmland, often by top-dressing planes. In this rural context it can also be a verb: to super a paddock means to fertilise it.

superette A medium-sized general store, gentrification of the terms corner store, dairy or general store.

swag of Plenty, an abundance of, a great quantity. The word is based on the image of a swag in its sense of backpack. *There were dozens of mushrooms in the paddock over the fence and we picked a whole swag of them.*

Swanndri (Swannie) Officially a bush shirt, a knee-length outdoor garment, sometimes hooded, loose fitting, made from woollen fabric which is waterproofed. The name of this New Zealand icon, now made in China, is actually a company trademark dating from 1913, believed to have been a mistaken spelling of swan + dry: the logo shows a swan.
(See **bush nightie**)

swede A nutritious root vegetable with dense yellow flesh and a characteristic, though not always popular, taste. Originally introduced into Scotland from Sweden, hence the name, it is known elsewhere as rutabaga, or sometimes neeps (which is strictly a turnip).

sweet as Shortened form of a complete phrase of comparison, such as sweet as honey, pie, sugar. *The holiday in Fiji was wonderful: great weather, delicious food and absolutely no stress. Sweet as.*

swifty / swiftie, pulling a Deceiving someone, being deceitful. Derived from swift, as in a quick movement, swifty or swiftie appears to have its origins in the navy, where a slow-moving rating was ironically described as a swiftie and by the mid-20th century the term had shifted into general use, with a connotation of being tricky and deceitful.

The practice of advertising air fares which seem impressively low, but do not include such extras as obligatory taxes, security and fuel costs and airport charges, would be described as pulling a swifty.
(See **quickie**)

swing the lead Avoiding work through being idle and

malingering; not fulfilling a commitment. The term is related to the shipboard task of sounding depths by swinging the lead of a plumb line. This was perceived as an easy job done with minimum effort, compared with more arduous tasks, so the leadsman was regarded as being less active than his fellows.

T

ta *abbrev.* of thank you. Used in Britain since the 18th century, where it is regarded as baby talk, ta is quite commonly used informally by New Zealand adults.

TAB *abbrev.* of Totalisator Agency Board. The 1949 New Zealand Gaming Amendment Act legalised off-course betting on horse-racing, and by March 1951 the first TABs began operating. The meaning of the term TAB soon moved to mean not the controlling board, but the various suburban offices at which bets could be placed. The TAB has evolved beyond horse-racing and now accepts bets on all types of national and international sport.

taha Maori *Maori* Doing things in the traditional way seen as significant to Maori. Taha Maori is an all-embracing term including knowledge of protocol, music and dance, legends, philosophical attitude and relationships. Taha can also designate a side or a slant, the perspective of an object, or a container.

tahi, rua, toru, wha *Maori* One, two, three, four. Often heard rhythmically spoken just before the start of a Maori performance item, so that the performers begin in synchronised tempo.

taiaha *Maori* A tall slender weapon made from wood, often decoratively carved and with an accessory fringe of feathers. Traditionally used for thrusting and battering, rather than spearing, it is still the focus of very skilful displays of such manipulation.

taihoa *Maori* Hold back, wait, suspend activity. Occasionally used inside an otherwise English sentence, as in a *New Zealand Herald* headline in 2005: 'Voters tell Tamihere to taihoa'.

takahe *Maori* A flightless tussock-dwelling bird, *Notornis mantelli*, believed to be extinct after 1900 but rediscovered by Dr G.B. Orbell in Fiordland in 1948. A short-legged plump bird with dark blue plumage and a characteristic red beak, the takahe looks a bit like a pukeko. Because imported deer eat the tussock on whose seeds the takahe relies, and stoats eat the bird's eggs and chicks, takahe are now protected in reserves.

takeaway Prepared food, packaged at the point of sale and eaten elsewhere. Other cultures refer to this food as 'take out', or 'to go'.

talk the leg off an iron pot The ability to speak seemingly without end, being long-winded. The term is ancient and based entirely on nonsense concepts: iron pot is only one of a string of such images, including talk the hind leg off a donkey, a dog, a brass pan and a horse. *It's hard to get away from Jen's mother – she can talk the leg off an iron pot.*

Tall Blacks Since 1990, the name for New Zealand's representative men's basketball team.

Tall Ferns Since 1999, the name for New Zealand's representative women's basketball team.

tall poppy, tall poppy syndrome A person of considerable success, a high-profile achiever. The term originated in Australia about 1900 but became prominent after 1931 when a politician referred to a tax that would cut the heads off the tall poppies (i.e. the wealthy). The term has widened to include the successful and prominent in a range of fields, sometimes also called big noters or people with their heads sticking above the parapets. The tall poppy syndrome refers to a common Australasian disdain for and suspicion of such people. As a verb, tall poppy means to ensure that someone is cut down to size.

tamaiti (*pl.* **tamariki**) *Maori* Child, children.

tamarillo An egg-shaped fruit with a deep red skin, yellow flesh and a highly characteristic flavour. The fruit is found in the Andes, from where New Zealand's first seeds came in 1891. From the 1920s onwards, the fruit became immensely popular in New Zealand, under the name tree tomato; in 1967 this was replaced by the invented name tamarillo. In the 1980s a yellow-skinned variety, the golden tamarillo, was developed in New Zealand.

tanalised Trade name for a method of treating timber against rot and insect damage. Treatment mixtures involve proportions of copper, chrome and arsenic, which allow the timber to combat breakdown and infestation.

Tangaroa *Maori* A god of the sea, part of the pre-European belief in a variety of gods who governed the natural world – a belief not entirely discarded, even after the arrival and embracing of Christianity.

tangata whenua *Maori* The people of the land, the indigenous inhabitants, a way of distinguishing Maori from all others.

tangi *Maori* The mourning ritual for and subsequent burial of someone who has recently died. The occasion is different in both structure and intent from what Europeans would customarily identify as a funeral. Correctly called tangihanga, Maori funeral rites can occupy several days, with the deceased's body lying surrounded by family, while relatives and friends, some of whom have travelled long distances, are formally welcomed in groups as they arrive.

taniko *Maori* A woven design on the edge of a garment. This can vary from tribe to tribe or can follow a universal design. Women's taniko bodices worn during cultural performances are highly prized, as are men's taniko belts.

taniwha *Maori* A legendary monster, often water-dwelling, whose presence is acknowledged in many traditional stories.

taonga *Maori* A treasure. A taonga can be something animate or inanimate – a precious stone, a person, an artefact, even a piece of land, native trees and birds – or something ephemeral such as a tradition or a prayer.

tap The valve that controls a fluid flow, elsewhere often called a faucet.

tapa A non-woven cloth made in some Pacific Islands. It consists of lengths of mulberry tree bark laid in overlapping sections, then moistened and beaten until the joins amalgamate. In its original condition, the extended length of 'fabric' is creamy-white in colour. It is customarily given an all-over rust-brown tint from a natural tree juice, and then decorated in designs of black. Very occasionally, a colour other than brown or black might be applied. An artificial version – woven cotton cloth decorated with 'tapa-like' designs – appears in many colours, at variance with the traditional commodity made from bark.

Tapanui flu Myalgic encephalomyelitis, also called chronic fatigue syndrome. This serious flu-like illness hit the news in New Zealand during the 1970s, when attention was drawn to the Otago town of Tapanui, where an unusual number of sufferers were located.

tapu *Maori* The prohibition of an action, or the use of an object, based on ritualistic distinctions of their being sacred and consecrated, or dangerous, unclean and accursed. The word is related to the Tongan original *tabu,* first heard by English-speaking people in 1770. Tapu and taboo do not have the same meaning: tapu indicates that something is restricted because it is sacred or connected with a spiritual matter; taboo often tends to mean simply forbidden, sometimes for moral rather than religious reasons. *This land has been tapu since the villagers were massacred here in the 1860s.*

Taranaki gate A rough-and-ready but efficient sticks-and-wire construction which serves as a gate, though it is actually a separate section of the fence hinged with wire loops at one end, and secured by wire loops at the other end, so it can be opened and shut. Usually they consist of three or four vertical wooden battens held together by horizontal strands of wire, often barbed. Despite its name, this kind of gate is used throughout New Zealand. The term was probably in use long before it appeared in print in 1937.

Taranaki salute Gumboots being stamped in order to shake off cow dung (which itself is known as Taranaki top dressing). Other local expressions from this lush and lovely dairying province include Taranaki sunshine (rain and drizzle), Taranaki violins (the sound of cow-bells) and Taranaki drive (a method of felling one tree deliberately so it falls on another and eventually results in several trees falling).

Taranaki wool A kind of fungus that grows on rotting logs. Huge amounts were exported to China in the 1870s by a New Plymouth merchant and entrepreneur named Chew Chong, who later turned his attention to New Zealand butter. He sent a shipment of this to Britain in 1885, and is thus credited with starting New Zealand's dairy export industry.

taro A large-leafed tropical plant (*Colocasia esculenta*) approximately 1 metre tall, grown on many of the Pacific islands. Its leaves and stems are often toxic but its large roots, cooked in various ways, provide a staple carbohydrate food.

ta-ta Informal way of saying goodbye, usually said by children or women. Men seldom use the term.

tatt, tatty Something of little value, shoddy or untidy, goods either worthless or in some way having been devalued by fashion or use or lack of attention. The origin is a Scottish dialect word, thought to be from the Old English *taettac*, meaning shredded, tattered.

tauiwi *Maori* The Maori word for non-Maori people. It is not

as commonly heard as *Pakeha* but is less controversial.
(See **Pakeha**)

te *Maori* The definite article *the*. Maori contains two versions of the definite article: te refers to a single object or concept, and nga refers to two or more.

tea The main evening meal, also known as dinner.

tea towel A cloth used for drying crockery, cutlery and kitchen utensils, when they have been washed after use.

tekoteko *Maori* A large wooden support pillar within a meeting house which is given character by having symbolic carved figures added to it.
(See **wharenui**)

tena koe, tena korua, tena koutou (katoa) *Maori* The greetings respectively spoken once for one person (tena koe), twice if greeting two people (tena korua, tena korua) or three times for a group of three or more (tena koutou, tena koutou, tena koutou) sometimes adding katoa, meaning all.

te reo See **reo, te**

Te Wai Pounamu *Maori* The Maori name for the South Island of New Zealand.

that'll be the day Exclamation expressing disbelief, lack of agreement or gross improbability.

that'll be (the phone) A nonsense phrase announcing the obvious, immediately after it has happened. The gimmick began as a running joke in the 1974 New Zealand television serial *Buck House*.

there you go A common expression of acknowledgement, roughly equivalent to the French *voilà* or Italian *ecco*. It can signify: here you are (handing someone a drink), how surprising! (when told something alarming), I'm listening to you but I don't agree, or isn't that what you'd expect to happen!

Thermette A narrow metal cylinder which holds water, which is quickly heated to boiling point by burning newspapers or twigs in a central tubular 'chimney'. The Thermette is used for picnicking and camping, and in North Africa during the Second World War it was known as a Benghazi boiler or burner. A New Zealand invention dating from the late 1920s, the rapid boiler was patented in 1936 under the trade name Thermette.

thrashing Overusing, overworking, stretching to maximum capacity. Besides punishment, or lunging about in a random manner, this New Zealand meaning for the word can refer to a vehicle such as a tractor or a car being given a thrashing, i.e. driven relentlessly or at high speed, to a bush area that has been overhunted, or to an argument or political policy that has been discussed exhaustively, even argumentatively. A complete, comprehensive thrashing is, oddly, described as good.

throw a wobbly To lose control, display bad temper, generally have a tantrum. The expression, which became common in New Zealand during the 1960s, appears to be just an economical verbal description of the behaviour involved. It would seem that wobbly has replaced fit in the similar and older expression, throw a fit. *For goodness sake don't park your car in Darryn's space. He'll throw a massive wobbly and embarrass everybody.*

thud, to come a To suffer a major failure, through bad luck or through having made a mistake in judgement.

tickets on, to have (1) A feeling of romantic affection towards someone, whether or not reciprocated. (2) To hold a person in regard, usually another person but sometimes oneself —which is commented on in a derogatory manner by others. *I'm sure Freda has tickets on young Andrew, but she's wasting her time – he's only got tickets on himself.*

tiger Someone who is enthusiastic and eager, usually for work, or for high standards. The expression is sometimes heard in what appears to be a contradictory sense: a tiger for punishment. This denotes that the person is ready and willing to take on complex projects and to work hard.

tight as a duck's arse Keeping a firm hold on money. The duck is sometimes replaced by a camel, but other comparisons for tightness include a full tick, a drum, a tennis racquet, a coffin or a bottom smile.

tikanga Maori *Maori* Habits, reasons and information regarded as an integral part of Maori life and its customary rights. The expression can be translated as 'culture'.

tiki *Maori* A stylised, almost foetal, human figure unique to Maori art, often depicted on a piece of jewellery, especially a pendant. In Maori legend, Tiki is the name for the Creator of Man, so one connotation of a tiki is that it represents the first man, and therefore one's ancestors. The figure's full, correct name is hei-tiki, but the shorter version is acceptable in informal situations.

tiki tour To take a long unnecessarily complicated route. Tiki Tours is the name of a perfectly respectable package-travel organisation, but the name has also acquired a common secondary meaning, as a result of the company's long, complex journeys. Later, and not at all connected to the firm, tiki tour came to mean either a long and unnecessarily complicated route or a route that is purposely lengthened to the disadvantage of the passenger, for instance by a taxi driver trying to make more money.

tin The tin can in which baked beans, preserved fruits etc. are sold. Overseas it is usually called a can, and while this usage is on the increase in New Zealand, it is still frequently called a tin, and the goods in it are therefore tinned. The usage extends to beer when sold in similar containers – a cylindrical container of beer is sometimes referred to as a tinnie, occasionally as a tube or a can.

tin-canning, tin-kettling   A social custom involving members of the community, usually rural, armed with empty tins, metal plates, dishes and spoons, making a great deal of supposedly joyous noise – related to the old German tradition of *Polter Abend* (noisy night). The ambulant band proceeds through the settlement, making noisy celebration either on Christmas Eve or New Year's Eve. In Australasia, the custom usually relates to a wedding, when the communal banging of tins etc. may take place around the bridal house the night before a wedding, or after the reception when the couple departs for a honeymoon – or most commonly after the honeymoon on their first night together in their dwelling, the noisy visit being seen as a welcome to the district from community and neighbours.

tinnie   A can of beer.
(See **tin**)

tinny   (1) Cheaply made, inefficient, lacking stability, hence tin-pot (based on the image of a container made of metal so thin that it crumples) and tin ear (tone deaf). (2) Small amounts of marijuana wrapped in silver foil, distributed from a tinny house. (3) Lucky, applied to a person who falls into advantage, apparently without effort. Extended references to such people include tin-bum or tin-arse.

tino rangatiratanga   *Maori* Complete rule by chieftainship, over land and everything on it. Sometimes called sovereignty.

tip   An area put aside where rubbish is placed, or tipped, sometimes known elsewhere as a garbage dump. No tipping (i.e. no rubbish dumping) signs can confuse visitors, who think they are instructions about gratuities for waiters.

tipuna   *Maori* Also known as tupuna: the variation

stems from differing tribal dialects. Ancestor (sometimes grandparent). The acknowledgement of ancestors figures prominently in Maori philosophy, prayer, song and beliefs.

tiwakawaka *Maori* See **fantail**

toby The encased tap and valve in a domestic water supply, at the junction of a property and the public road. The word comes from *tobar* in the Irish Shelta language, meaning road. In English, as high toby, it came to refer to robbery on the highway and sometimes a highwayman was referred to as a tobyman. The terms probably came to New Zealand with early settlers and the meaning somehow transferred from the road itself to the water-main tap installed on the road. Very occasionally toby refers to a gas mains tap.

toey Nervously on edge, and sometimes irritable as well. The image originated with horses on alert, toeing the ground with a hoof. Americans would say antsy. *The restaurant was fairly full and service was slow, which was a bit of a worry because Joseph can get really toey if he doesn't get his food quickly.*

togs Garment especially worn for swimming. The word is directly derived from the Latin word *toga*. Another word for togs is swimming costume, in Australia your cossie or your swimmers.

toheroa *Maori* An indigenous clam-like shellfish (*Amphidesma ventricosum*) which can burrow deeply into beach sand. Their flavour is much prized, particularly in a chowder, but because of former excessive harvesting, collection is strictly controlled by law.

tohunga *Maori* A priest-like figure, usually advanced in years, and with a deep knowledge of healing, prayers and philosophy. The term can also designate a person with special expertise in a specific subject. Tohunga has sometimes been quite incorrectly translated as medicine man, which gives a completely wrong connotation. For many years tohunga activities were forbidden by law, until the legislation was repealed in 1962.

toilet (1) Lavatory. (2) Down the toilet – see **down the tubes**.

tonky Suggesting plutocratic tendencies, elitism by virtue of money, or superiority of thought and action because of niche sporting activity and interests considered ephemeral by some. The word is thought to be a combination of tony and swanky.

too right Very positive affirmation, emphasised agreement. *Are you still planning to come with us to the cricket? Too right!*

top dressing Often used as an abbreviation for aerial top-dressing or the spreading of fertiliser by low-flying plane equipped with hoppers. This is a New Zealand invention and the first such flight, which actually distributed pasture seed, took place in 1936. Some countries call it crop-dusting.

top shelf High in esteem or position. This is a compliment to be earned and is not automatically assigned to those whose eminence rests on wealth or rank. The image comes from a bar where the more expensive spirits, liqueurs and other specialist drinks are kept on the top shelf.

toss the lollies, tiger, meal To vomit. The images refer variously to the strong desire to vomit (the tiger), the colour and texture produced (the lollies) or simply to what is actually being vomited (the meal).

totara *Maori* An impressive forest tree (*Podocarpus totara*) with beautiful wood. Diseased portions of the wood produce complex patterns within the grain which are especially prized for decorative cabinet-making.

towie *abbrev.* of tow-truck driver, or the truck itself. Towies appear at an accident to remove the wreckage or a damaged car, or when a serious parking offence has been discovered and the offending vehicle is taken to an impounding area.

tracksuit Loose-fitting pants and a jacket, usually zipped, often in medium-weight knit fabric, originally intended for athletes to wear before and after participating in a strenuous sporting event. Now, however, tracksuits are worn by almost everyone, regardless of age, gender and activity. Elsewhere tracksuits are known as sweats, trackies or le training.

trailers (1) The short piece of film showing highlights from a forthcoming movie which is shown before the main feature. Trailers used to be called shorts. Originally trailers were shown after the current film, giving highlights of the following week's movie, hence the name. The movie industry now tends to use the terms teaser or promo. (2) A wheeled conveyance of varying size drawn behind a car or truck. Unlike its American equivalent, a New Zealand trailer is not usually intended for travelling or sleeping in.
(See **shorts**)

tranny (1) *abbrev.* of either transvestite (usually a male who customarily dresses and presents as a woman) or transsexual (a person who has undergone radical surgery, as a result of which they are categorised as having changed sex). (2) A transistor radio.

tree   See **out of one's tree**

troppo, to go   To become irrational and out of touch with reality. Based on an abbreviation of tropical, the term originated among the military in the Pacific area during the Second World War, when men became unstable after a long time in the hot climate. The term was retained in general use to describe a perceived period of mental instability. *David's going troppo in there. Just because sales are down this month, I don't see why he has to take it out on us.*

trots (1) *abbrev.* of a race meeting for trotters, pacers and harness racers. (2) Diarrhoea.

trundler A small hand-propelled vehicle, sometimes two-wheeled, for convenient carrying of sports equipment, supermarket shopping, or a small child.

tuatara A native reptile which resembles a lizard, but is in fact the only survivor in the world of a separate species of reptile, *Rhynchocephalia*, which lived 200 million years ago. Except for the tuatara, the species became extinct 100 million years ago. Each individual is thought to live for 200 years or more. The first one seen by a European, John Gray, was in 1831, and that one might still be alive in 2031. The creature's forehead is characterised by a small depression, sometimes called a vestige of a third eye, which contains nerve-ends, probably for heat-sensing. The slow-moving tuatara has not coped well with imported mammals and can now only live safely on predator-free islands.

tui *Maori* A native bird (*Prosthemadera novaeseelandiae*) with notably glossy black plumage and a characteristic cluster of curved white feathers at its throat. The tui, which eats nectar and tree fruits, has a beautiful and carrying song. In city districts with plenty of trees, it will come right into suburban gardens. It was known as the parson bird because of the feathers at its throat.

tukus A slang term for men's underpants, originating from a 1997 financial scandal when New Zealand's first all-Maori television channel fell into major debt through financial misadventures, and it was alleged that a director, Tukoroirangi Morgan, besides other extravagances, had bought extremely expensive underwear, allegedly with business funds. The resultant term, tukus, is now also occasionally applied to doubtful spending of any kind.

tukutuku *Maori* A style of criss-cross weaving using flat flexible 'slats' of plant material, often seen on the walls of a wharenui.

tupuna See **tipuna**

turangawaewae *Maori* Ancestral lands, a strong feeling of affinity someone feels for the territory which was traditionally the home of their tribe. The literal meaning is a 'place to stand'.

turn it in To finish early, relinquish responsibility, give up.

turn it up Agreement to, and possible willingness for, sexual activity.

tutae *Maori* Excrement. The word has occurred in two place-names, the translation for which has caused brows to furrow. Colonists making a settlement in the Rangitikei area in 1859 found that the position chosen had the name Tutaenui. The colonists were not completely comfortable when they discovered that Tutaenui meant big turd. In 1869, the decision was made to re-name the town after the birthplace of Captain Cook, and it became Marton. Much later, on a visit to Hawke's Bay, it was reported that the Queen asked what the Tutaekuri River meant in translation, and a red-faced official had to tell her it meant dog turds.

two-up A game involving a mild form of betting, when two coins are thrown up and bets are placed on whether they will both fall heads or tails.

tyre kicker A person who skirts around or talks a great deal about an issue or a prospect, without ever committing themselves to involvement. The image arises from car sales yards, where visitors spend a lot of time examining the vehicles but do not buy.

U

underground mutton Cooked rabbit. Rabbits were introduced into New Zealand in 1838, to provide meat for the settlers, but soon proliferated to become a menace, especially in the South Island. Rabbit meat went out of fashion completely during most of the 20th century, until the health-conscious became alerted to its lean qualities, and interest began again.

uni *abbrev.* of university. This is a recent New Zealand adoption from Australian usage.
(See **varsity**)

unit title The legal title to ownership of a dwelling (unit) but not to the land it stands on.

untold An expression of quantity indicating that there is no limit to the amount of whatever is being so described, but customarily used fancifully and casually with scant regard for accuracy.

unwaged A deliberately coined word which, besides the unemployed, includes the retired, at-home mothers, students, the disabled and sickness beneficiaries – anyone who does not actually earn a wage. A special unwaged price can be advertised for show tickets and transport.

up the booai (boohai) A long way from cities and business districts, out of the mainstream. During the 19th century immigrants arrived in Auckland from the region of Czechoslovakia then known as Bohemia and almost all settled to the north at the then distant rural district of Puhoi. The name came to mean faraway, the back of beyond, and the pronunciation altered to Booai. The up came a little later, in such silly phrases as 'up the booai for the rhubarb season'.

urupa *Maori* A burial ground. The term encompasses both pre-colonial burial areas, and the more modern concept of cemetery.

uruwhenua *Maori* Passport. A created word, uruwhenua can be translated as homeland. Maori is an official language in New Zealand and is therefore included on all such documents.

use one's block To concentrate, show good sense and reasoning.
(See **block, do your block, knock someone's block off**)

ute *abbrev.* for a utility, a small but feisty truck. Known elsewhere as a pick-up truck.

utu *Maori* To engage in and succeed in an act of utu means that satisfaction has been achieved, possibly over a wrong righted, or a return, a reward, even a compensation. The word is frequently translated into English as revenge, but that fails to give the full picture, as carrying out utu does not always involve violence. It is harsh when the original action being righted was in itself harsh.

V

varsity *abbrev.* for university.

Vegemite An all-vegetable mix also including yeast used as a sandwich spread. An icon of the New Zealand kitchen cupboard, with a unique flavour, it is part of the nation's culinary landscape and New Zealanders take it with them on their OE. Vegemite was invented by an industrial chemist in Melbourne, who was working on ways of improving brewer's yeast. It has been made in Australia since 1925 and in New Zealand since 1958. The name was the result of a competition. In 2004 New Zealanders bought 2.2 million jars of Vegemite.

veggies *abbrev.* for vegetables.

vid *abbrev.* for video, usually meaning a videotape, rather than the machine on which you play it.

W

wahine *Maori* Woman, wife.

wai *Maori* Water. The term occurs in many placenames where water is a feature of the area named, but the word also has a connotation of flow and can be found in terms that do not include actual water, e.g. waiata (song), which literally means 'a shape that flows'.

wairua *Maori* The inner being, the spirit, the life force.

waka *Maori* Usually translated as canoe, though it actually means container, the different applications being obvious by the context. As a canoe, a waka can be anything from a modest inshore dugout to a big ocean-going vessel.

wakahuia *Maori* A small box, usually beautifully carved and decorated, originally intended to hold precious decorative bird feathers. Wakahuia were prized possessions of rangatira.

waka jumper Literally, someone who jumps from one canoe to another, but it has become a metaphor for a politician who abandons the party that initially brought him or her into Parliament. By extension, the term can refer to anyone who leaves an organisation with which they have become identified, and moves to a different (possibly rival) group – usually to their own advantage.

walk off To leave employment, family responsibilities, a farmer's unprofitable land, sometimes precipitately, and with no intention of returning.

wampo, on the Slang term popularised by the Royal Air Force for a drinking session with alcohol, usually beer. The term is thought to be derived from a Scottish dialect word meaning to wave the arms about.

wananga, whare wananga *Maori* Basically a meeting but, by extension (and adding whare) the building where a meeting will be held. Whare wananga can also designate a house of learning.

wearable art As the expression suggests, dazzling and beautiful garments that are artworks rather than clothes. The annual World of Wearable Art presentation, begun in 1987 in Nelson and now based in Wellington, has grown to become one of the greatest theatre spectacles staged in New Zealand, showing that artistic inspiration and skill can create spectacular art which is displayed on the human body rather than a wall or a pedestal.

weatherboard (1) A system of building whereby the outside walls consist of narrow timbers, laid horizontally one overlapping the other. (2) A device at the bottom of a door opening to an outside area, which on closure, swings down and prevents entry of rain or winds.

weekender Term used by residents of a rural district with scenic attractions to describe householders who live and work in distant, usually urban, places, and come to stay just at weekends.

weka *Maori* A hen-sized flightless bird (*Gallirallus australis*), brownish speckled with black, noted for its discreet curiosity and rather bold visits to camping sites and houses.

wero *Maori* A ceremonial challenge, to a site – usually a tribal territory such as a marae – where the group belonging to the area confront a visitor with challenges and rituals before welcoming them to enter. In contemporary times the challenge quotient is solely ritual, but is nevertheless strictly observed as an integral part of the welcome ceremony. A wero can also be styled to challenge a person to achieve, to carry out a task, to face life.

Westies Strictly, people living in the western (Waitakere) area of Greater Auckland. The term originated in Sydney in the 1970s when people in the eastern suburbs regarded people in the western suburbs as socially disadvantaged. The term has become moderately familiar in New Zealand, although cities without clearly defined east–west orientation tend to use the word bogan instead. Westies are proud of their laid-back lifestyle and working-class culture, and were celebrated by Waitakere mayor Bob Harvey in his book *Westies* (2004).

weta *Maori* An insect of significant size, flightless, with a shiny exoskeleton which is usually a glossy brown, and formidable-looking spiny legs.

wet hen, silly as a A dithering indecisive person, perhaps given to much chatter but little effective action. The image is based, somewhat unfairly, on the fact that hens, when they become very wet, lose dignity and become squawking scramblers. *Don't ever rely on her – she really is as silly as a wet hen.*

whack See **out of whack**

whack into To initiate a fight, attack vigorously.

whack up To make quickly, to carry out a task with little warning or preparation.

whaddarya? An informal rhetorical question, delivered contemptuously and plainly signifying that the questioner will not agree or approve of the reply, whatever it is. It first became prominent in the 1980 play *Foreskin's Lament* by Greg McGee, when addressed to a character who dares to challenge the supremacy of rugby over life's other activities.

whaka blonde (1) A Maori woman, who by nature would have black hair. (2) Any woman with naturally black hair who has become blonde by chemistry.

whakapapa *Maori* The simple translation is genealogy, but in Maori terms a diagrammatic structure of a person's heritage might not confine itself solely to blood descent, but follow the macro-outline of a family structure, including connections to other families, and even to the land.

whanau *Maori* Family. This would include not just a nuclear family of mother, father and children, but also the extended family of grandparents, uncles and aunts, cousins and in-laws.

whare *Maori* House or building. If the latter, a qualifying suffix would designate the building's purpose, e.g. whare kai – communal hall where food is served, whare puni – a large room for visitors to sleep, whare kura – a house of learning, a school.

wharenui *Maori* An impressive central building in a marae, the front portion of which invariably forms a backdrop to the formal ceremonies of wero and powhiri.
(See **marae**)

wharfie Informal term for waterside worker, wharf labourer, longshoreman.

Wheel Blacks New Zealand's national representative wheelchair rugby team.

whenua *Maori* Land – not just the grounds of a building or the area of a park, but the concept of land as the whole country itself.

whio *Maori* A blue duck *(Hymenolaimus malacorhynchus)* which can cope with rough mountain waters, and emits a strange whistle-like call that gives the bird its Maori name, which means whistle.

White Ferns New Zealand international women's cricket team. Early teams of women cricketers representing New Zealand internationally, starting in 1935, were known simply as the New Zealand Women's Cricket team. The name White Ferns was adopted formally in 2000, the year the New Zealand team won the women's Cricket World Cup.

White Sox The New Zealand international women's softball team. Women's softball teams, which have played internationally from 1949, had no special name until the name White Sox was adopted for the women in 2000, following the name Black Sox being adopted for the men's team in 1997.

windy Scared, nervous, lacking courage. (See **get the wind up**)

winebox A collective term for any group of documents which, if examined properly, could expose an actual or potential fraud. The word is based on an incident in 1994 when documents concerning taxes in relation to overseas investments were delivered into the debating chamber in a cardboard wine-bottle carton.

wobbly See **throw a wobbly**

woolly woofter (1) A male homosexual. (2) Anyone else perceived by laboriously macho men as having sensibilities and interests beyond rugby, racing and beer.

wopcacker Impressive, outstanding, surprising. The term originated in Australia in the 1920s, combining elements of whopper and cracker-jack. There have been various spellings – whopcacker, woopcacker, even woopknacker – but since the word is not a formal part of the language none of these variations matters.

wops, wop-wops Remote, distant rural areas. Early British settlers to Australia, amused by the number of Aboriginal placenames with repeated or similar-sounding syllables (e.g. Waggawagga), made up the word woop-woops as a satirical mock-native word. New Zealanders very soon adopted the word, using it to mean a place so distant that it has no real name, though they pronounced it with shorter vowels.

wowser A person who appears to be disgruntled at the

pleasures of others, is stoically pious and attempts to force their own morality on people not necessarily in sympathy with them. The word appeared to come to life in 1899 when John Norton, editor of Australia's *Truth*, claimed to have invented it, referring to an alderman as 'the white, woolly, weary, watery, word-wasting wowser from Waverley'. It later became associated with the slogan 'We Only Want Social Evils Remedied' but some scholars suggest that wowser might stem from an English dialect reference to a dog whining.

Y

yakka   See **hard yakka**

yakking   Talk perceived by an observer as non-productive. The word arose from a 1930s American slang term, yocking, which meant useless talk. The term went through various versions until by 1958 it became yakking, or yackety yak – idle chatter or empty babble. The word may have some ancestor in Yiddish, but is commonly regarded as having an echoic origin. New Zealanders quickly caught on to the word and it is still in common use.

Another similar term is the much older (1918) *blah-di-blah-di-blah,* a possible corruption of the German *blech* (nonsense). During the 1990s the popular television show *Seinfeld* engendered a new version of the same idea: *yadda-yadda-yadda.*

ya' reckon?   To query, as in: is that your considered opinion? Based on its meaning of calculate, the word reckon has taken on several shades of meaning in New Zealand, often as a statement of confident personal opinion rather than reasoned belief. Cockney English, with its endearing habit of spicing ordinary talk with rather grand terms, has used reckon for years, but usually in the negative: I don't reckon it'll work. New Zealanders customarily use the word in both negative and positive contexts.

yonks   An indefinitely long time. The term, widely used in New Zealand, was first noticed in the British Army in the 1950s. The word is thought to be either a cryptic combination of years, months and weeks or a sloppy contraction of donkeys' years, meaning a long time because the animal's ears are long.

youse   Informal – second person plural. English does not have a specific formal word for this part of speech, so some people gradually developed the possible but non-standard candidate, youse, meaning that several people are being addressed.

yummy Food that is tasty. Derived from yum-yum and usually regarded as a childlike description, yummy has become moderately acceptable for adult usage in New Zealand and is often heard in conversation and from cooks on television.

Z

Zambuck Members of the St John Ambulance organisation, who are a familiar sight at sports matches and public events, where they offer paramedical attention if needed. Although the word zambuck could possibly have arisen as a corruption of St Johns Ambulance, its origin is more likely to be the ointment they used, called Zambuck, popular in New Zealand since 1900.

Zespri Kiwifruit. This name was coined in 1997 when the New Zealand Kiwifruit Marketing Board decided a rebranding was needed. Zespri was chosen for its crisp sound and is now used to market the fruit internationally.
(See **kiwifruit**)

Zip Proprietary name for a domestic water heater, the name often being used as shorthand in referring to the appliance. Zip was registered as a trade name in 1933 by Maunder Ltd, Wellington.

zorb A large, very strong transparent ball, with a slightly smaller, equally strong transparent ball secured inside it. As a novelty activity, a person enters the inner sphere and is then rolled down a slope, where the sphere's speed can reach 50 kilometres per hour. Apart from adventures with gravity, the passenger is protected by the cushion of air between the two spheres. The name is an invented word.

Acronyms commonly used in New Zealand

AA – Automobile Association
ACC – Accident Compensation Corporation
ACT (political party) – Association of Consumers and Tax Payers
A & E – Accident and Emergency
AI – Artificial Insemination
ALAC – Alcohol Advisory Council
APEC – Asia-Pacific Economic Cooperation
CAB – Citizens' Advice Bureau
CCU – Coronary Care Unit
CD – Civil Defence
CROC – Crown-owned Company
CTU – Council of Trade Unions
DOC – Department of Conservation
DHB – District Health Board
ECT – Electro-convulsive Therapy
ENT – Ear, Nose and Throat
DPB – Domestic Purposes Benefit
EFTPOS – Electronic Transfer of Funds at Point of Sale
ERMA – Environmental Risk Management Authority
ERO – Educational Review Office
ESOL – English for Speakers of Other Languages
FPP – First Past the Post (electoral system)
GATT – General Agreement on Trade and Tariffs
GDP – Gross Domestic Product
GM – Genetically Modified
GNP – Gross National Product
GP – General Practitioner
GST – Goods and Services Tax
HR – Human Resources

HSBC – Hong Kong and Singapore Banking Corporation
IMF – International Monetary Fund
IRD – Inland Revenue Department
JP – Justice of the Peace
LIM – Land Information Memorandum
LINZ – Land Information New Zealand
LMVD – Licensed Motor Vehicle Distributor
MAF – Ministry of Agriculture and Forestry
MFAT – Ministry of Foreign Affairs and Trade
MMP – Mixed Member Proportional Representation (electoral system)
MOH – Ministry of Health
MONZ – Museum of New Zealand
MOT – Ministry of Transport
MP – Member of (New Zealand) Parliament
NCEA – National Certificate of Educational Achievement
NCW – National Council of Women
NIWA – National Institute of Water and Atmospheric Research
NZDF – New Zealand Defence Force
OOS – Occupational Overuse Syndrome
OSH – Occupational Safety and Health
PI – Pacific Islander
PMS – Pest Management Strategy
PSA – Public Service Association
RMA – Resource Management Act
RSA – Returned Services Association
SOE – State-owned Enterprise
TAB – Totalisator Agency Board
WINZ – Work and Income New Zealand
WOF – Warrant of Fitness
WTO – World Trade Organisation

Bibliography

Acker, Arch, *New Zild and How to Speak It*. A.H. and A.W. Reed, 1966.

Bamett, Stephen and Richard Wolfe, *New Zealand! New Zealand! In Praise of Kiwiana*. Hodder & Stoughton, 1989.

Bamett, Stephen and Richard Wolfe, *Kiwiana! The Sequel*. Penguin, 2001.

Brewer's Dictionary of Modem Phrase and Fable, ed. Adrian Room. Cassell, 2000.

Brewer's Dictionary of Phrase and Fable, 15th edition, ed. Adrian Room. Cassell, 1996.

Brewer's Dictionary of Twentieth Century Phrase and Fable. Cassell, 1991.

Chapman, Robert L. (ed.), *The Dictionary of American Slang*. Harper Perennial, 1998.

Deverson, Tony & Graeme Kennedy (eds), *The New Zealand Oxford Dictionary*. Oxford University Press, 2005.

Ell, Gordon, *An A-Z of Kiwi Folklore*. New Holland, 2003.

MacAlistair, John (ed.), *A Dictionary of Maori Words in New Zealand English*. Oxford University Press, 2005.

McGill, David, *A Dictionary of Kiwi Slang*. Mills Publications, 1988.

McGill, David, *The Complete Kiwi Slang Dictionary*. Reed Publishing, 1998.

Morris, Edward E., *Austral English: A Dictionary of Australasian Words*. Macmillan, 1898.

Orange, Claudia (ed.), *The Dictionary of New Zealand Biography,* Volumes I-V. Auckland University Press, 2000.

Orsman, H.W. (ed.), *The Dictionary of New Zealand English*. Oxford University Press, 1997.

Orsman, H.W. (ed.), *A Dictionary of Modern New Zealand Slang*. Oxford University Press, 1999.

Partridge, Eric, *Origins: A Short Etymological Dictionary of Modern English*. Book Club Associates, 1959.

Partridge, Eric, *A Dictionary of Catch Phrases*. Routledge and Kegan Paul, 1977.

Partridge, Eric, *A Concise History of Slang and Unconventional English,* ed. Paul Beale. Routledge, 1992.

Reed, A.W., *The Reed Dictionary of New Zealand Place Names*, Reed Publishing, 2002.

Smith, Carl V., *From N to Z*. Hicks Smith & Wright, 1947.

Also by Max Cryer

Hear Our Voices, We Entreat
The extraordinary story of New Zealand's national anthems

New Zealand has two national anthems, 'God Save the Queen' and 'God Defend New Zealand', but it is the latter that has the more curious history. After enterprising Irish settler Thomas Bracken penned the words in 1876, he held a competition for people to compose the music. The winner was John Joseph Woods, an unknown schoolteacher from Lawrence, central Otago. The path to the song's acceptance as our national anthem was long and complicated; there were many rivals – over fifty other compositions purporting to be 'New Zealand's national song' were written and published during the next fifty years. But with a little help, 'God Defend New Zealand' gained the ascendancy, although it was not until 1972 that it was first heard – mysteriously and unofficially – as an anthem at an Olympic Games medal ceremony (when the rowing eight won gold). It took a further five years before it became an official national anthem.

Max Cryer tells the full story of the rise and fall of 'God Defend New Zealand', unearthing many fascinating and little-known facts, and correcting some popular misconceptions. Heavily illustrated, this delightful and timely book will enlighten, astonish and entertain.

ISBN 0 908988 35 4

EXISLE
PUBLISHING